FLORIDA
BACK ROADS

FLORIDA
BACK ROADS

▲ ▲ ▲

Bob Howard

A publication of
The Orlando Sentinel

Sentinel **C**ommunications **C**ompany
Orlando
1 ▲ 9 ▲ 9 ▲ 1

Copyright © 1991
Sentinel Communications Company
633 N. Orange Avenue, Orlando, Florida 32801

Edited By April K. Medina
Designed by Mary Ann Rosenthal

Cover photograph of Richard and Joanne Tate by Red Huber
Back cover photograph by Peggy McClintock
Map illustrations by Gerald Masters
Photographs courtesy of the Florida Department of Commerce,
Division of Tourism
Printed in the United States by R. R. Donnelley
First edition 1991

Library of Congress Cataloging-in-Publication Data
Howard, Robert, 1922-
   Florida back roads / by Robert Howard.
      p.   cm.
   "A publication of the Orlando sentinel. "
   Includes index.
   ISBN 0-941263-16-9
   1. Florida — Description and travel — 1981 — Guide-books.
2. Automobile travel — Florida — Guide-books. 3. Bicycle touring-
Florida — Guide-books.   I. Title.
F309.3H68   1991
917.5904'63 — dc20   91-24564
                                                                            CIP

About the Author

Most bikers start touring at a fairly young age. I was 57 when I decided the best way to see the countryside was from the seat of a bicycle. My first serious venture was in 1979. The event was RAGBRAI, a monstrous ride across Iowa sponsored by *The Des Moines Register* that attracts more than 10,000 cyclists each year. After making the 480-mile ride in one week, I was hooked.

In fact, RAGBRAI so impressed me that I convinced *The Orlando Sentinel* to start a similar ride in Florida. It was called the Sentinel Safari, and I headed it up all five years of its existence.

In the years since that first Safari I have ridden more than 30 tours of varying lengths. The longest was a ride of 4,600 miles across the United States when I was 65. That ride, which was a celebration of my retirement, took three months from Seattle to Bar Harbor, Maine. It was a self-contained ride—everything was on my bike, including a bedroll, tent, tools, clothes and pots and pans. Friends and relatives thought I was crazy, but I really got a close look at this country. I also have been on three-week tours of the Canadian Rockies and Maritime Provinces, along with many weeklong trips in Florida and points beyond.

Hopefully, there will be many more rides in the future. When I saw an 89-year-old man riding with the last Sentinel Safari, I was convinced cycling is a sport you never get too old to enjoy. There will always be at least one more road to explore and one more hill to climb.

Assisting in the selection of
routes were: Lys Burden of the
American Youth Hostels,
Bob Dioguardi, Russ Hurd
and Ernie Lambe.

Contents

Introduction

Exploring Florida is nothing new. It has been going on for more than 450 years, ever since Hernando De Soto and his men were slogging around the state in search of gold and other treasures.

Florida was the first part of the United States to be discovered by the white man, but centuries passed before it became settled.

And now that it is settled, it is time for another kind of exploring.

Nowadays the best way to really see a place is from the seat of a bicycle.

This book details 40 routes around the state that will let cyclists get a close look at Florida. From the Panhandle to the Everglades, from the Gulf to the ocean, cyclists will visit 55 of the state's 67 counties.

Despite the explosive growth since the early 1950s that placed Florida among the four most populous states, there still are many areas where there are few people and wonderfully quiet roads. This book will introduce you to those areas and guide you through them with easy-to-follow directions.

There are routes through the peanut and cotton fields of the Panhandle, along the white-as-snow beaches of the

Gulf, through the orange groves of Central Florida, the sugar cane fields of South Florida, around the second largest inland lake in the country, through the vast wilderness of the Everglades to the southernmost point on the U.S. mainland and along Atlantic beaches that few tourists ever visit.

You'll also visit many beautiful state parks on these routes — and you'll see them much the way the Indians did. You'll ride through small towns off the beaten track, tour historic sites, pedal around the oldest city in the United States and enjoy isolated villages.

Three old forts, battlefields from the Civil War and the Seminole Indian War, an old lighthouse, the oldest plantation house in Florida, an Indian reservation and three national forests are included in these expeditions.

Florida has a long and colorful history, and you'll learn about much of it on these tours.

Many of the routes are in North and Central Florida and in the Panhandle. Dense population and the accompanying traffic congestion make it difficult to enjoy bicycle touring in South Florida.

As you might expect, there are no rides involving Florida's major cities. Most of the routes are well-removed from population centers and away from the main highways.

Of the 40 routes, 18 can be handled in a single day; 11 can be biked in either one or two days. These longer routes have been planned so you can camp overnight or stay in a motel. Ten routes definitely require two days for all but the hardiest riders; one is planned for three days. Twelve of the routes can be coupled so you can enjoy two in one weekend.

There is more than just biking on these trips. There are chances to go swimming — either along the route or at the route's beginning or end. Choose from the Gulf, the Atlantic Ocean, scenic rivers, natural springs or lakes. You can rent canoes and small boats at several stops.

Many of the state parks have hiking trails that let you explore the wilderness and get a look at the great variety of small game, birds and waterfowl. Florida has outstanding state parks that usually are overlooked by most residents.

Before you start, know that an odometer is a must. The routes are described with exact mileage figures listed. Because many of the rides are through rural areas and in small counties, some roads are not marked or are so poorly marked they are easy to miss. You'll need the odometer to know where to turn. And remember that all odometers aren't created equal — some figures could be off by as much as a tenth of a mile.

Take a water bottle — better yet, take two. There are many routes where you can go for miles without being able to get a cold drink or refill you bottles — a real problem on hot days. Places where you'll find drinking water are indicated on the maps with a water drop symbol.

There are some steep hills — notably on routes out of Quincy and Zephyrhills — but this is Florida. Most of the terrain is either table-top flat or gently rolling.

Though this book is designed for bikers, tourists or Floridians who want to get better acquainted with their state might decide to climb in a car and take a look.

If you do, please watch out for the bikers.

So your book won't get damaged by carrying it with you on the various routes, it is suggested you photocopy the chapter of the route you plan on riding before you start.

1. Northwest (Panhandle)

▲ DeFuniak Springs-Graceville loop

A route that brings you within two miles of the Alabama border starts and ends in DeFuniak Springs and meanders across Walton, Holmes, Jackson and Washington counties for 107 miles.

You'll be in the Florida Panhandle, so you can look forward to quiet roads the entire way. There will be some good hills at the ride's start, but you'll cruise mostly rolling country. The roads — except for a few miles after you leave Graceville — are good.

This route is designed for two days with an overnight stop in Graceville. There is an eight-unit motel there. There are no campgrounds on the route, so there is no alternative to the Graceville motel if you choose to make this a two-day ride. The first day's ride is 54.4 miles, leaving about 53 miles for the second day. Because the terrain is easy to handle and there are no traffic problems, the route can be negotiated in a single day.

Leave your car beside the sheriff's office behind the Walton County Courthouse on 6th Street in DeFuniak Springs. You might want to alert the sheriff's office that your car is there.

You'll pedal a couple of miles on U.S. Highway 90 before heading into the rural sections east and north of DeFuniak Springs. Expect some hills here. The highest point in Florida is just a few miles off the route in the northern part of the county. It's 345 feet — not mountainous, but enough altitude to give you a change of pace from the routes along the Gulf beaches.

At the 9.6-mile mark on the ride, County Road 183 meets C.R. 183A and C.R. 183B. Turn left onto C.R. 183B. It's unmarked.

Soon after you enter Holmes County you'll turn onto State Road 2 and travel on that road for 28 miles, mostly through farming country, before you enter Graceville just inside the Jackson County line.

As you ride through the farms of Holmes County, you'll see fields devoted to peanuts, cotton and watermelon. The watermelon grown here is noted for its sweetness, and huge quantities are produced each summer for shipment to markets around the South.

There are no towns between DeFuniak Springs and Graceville, but there are several small stores on S.R. 2 that stock cold drinks and snacks.

Graceville is in the extreme northwest corner of Jackson County; it's less than two miles from the city limits to Alabama.

The farm country around Graceville and in Jackson County is similar to that in Holmes County — thousands of acres of peanut fields. This county is the largest peanut producer in the state.

You'll ride for more than 10 miles on C.R. 162 in Jackson and Holmes counties, and some of it is rough. Watch out for sand in the road — particularly in the curves.

Not long after the route returns to Holmes County you'll enter Bonifay, the county seat. Its population is about 2,000; the town is a trading center for area farmers.

You'll leave Bonifay on U.S. Highway 90. It parallels Interstate 10 a couple of miles to the south. Most of the east-west traffic is on that road. Only local traffic is on U.S. Highway 90, and it's extremely light. You'll be on this all the way back to DeFuniak Springs and the end of the route.

For about four miles after leaving Bonifay you'll be in Washington County and will ride through the town of Caryville. If you're making this a two-day trip, you'll have time to stop and browse in DeFuniak Springs.

You'll notice a small monument in front of the courthouse where you left your car. It's the first Confederate monument erected in Florida, placed there by the women of Walton County in 1871.

From the courthouse it's only a few blocks south to Lake DeFuniak. This round lake in the center of the town is encircled by impressive Victorian homes. A building constructed in 1909 for the Florida Chautauqua, a touring group, also is on the lake. The large wooden structure served as the home for the programs staged for the people of the Panhandle and southern Alabama until the Depression of the '30s.

Walton County — stretching from the Gulf of Mexico to Alabama — is the seventh largest county in the state, but much of it is occupied by Eglin Air Force Base. The

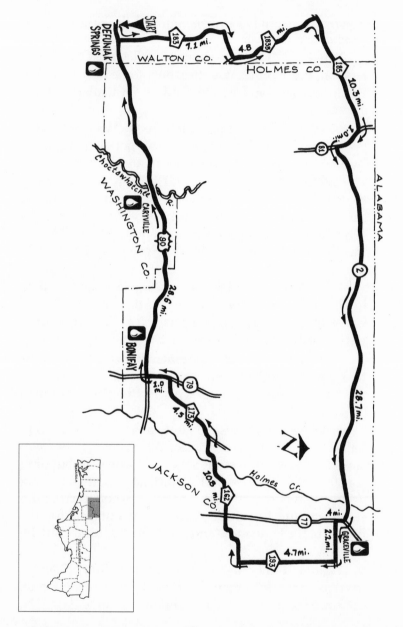

Air Force occupies all but a few acres from the Gulf to Interstate 10 through the middle of the county. The area you'll be riding through is north of Eglin.

The people in these four counties are genuine Southerners, friendly and easy to talk to. Most families have lived in the same place for several generations. Unlike so much of Florida, few newcomers are moving into this area.

DeFuniak Springs — Graceville loop:
1. Turn left from 6th Street next to courthouse onto U.S. Highway 90 and go 2.5 miles to C.R. 183.
2. Turn left on C.R. 183 and go 7.1 miles to C.R. 183A and C.R. 183B junction.
3. Turn left on C.R. 183B and go 4.8 miles to C.R. 185 (Moore's Cross Road).
4. Turn right on C.R. 185 and go 10.3 miles to S.R. 81.
5. Turn right on S.R. 81 and go 1 mile to S.R. 2.
6. Turn left on S.R. 2 and go 28.7 miles to S.R. 77 in Graceville.
7. Turn right on S.R. 77 and go four-tenths of a mile to S.R. 2.
8. Turn left on S.R. 2 and go 2.2 miles to C.R. 193 (Smokey Road).
9. Turn right on C.R. 193 and go 4.7 miles to C.R. 162.
10. Turn right on C.R. 162 and go 10.8 miles to C.R. 173.
11. Turn left on C.R. 173 and go 4.5 miles to S.R. 79 in Bonifay.
12. Turn left on S.R. 79 and go 1 mile to U.S. Highway 90.
13. Turn right on U.S. Highway 90 and go 28.6 miles to courthouse in DeFuniak Springs and end of route.

▲ Fort Pickens-Navarre Beach loop

One of the more interesting bicycle rides in Florida and certainly one with the most spectacular view of the Gulf of Mexico is on Santa Rosa Island in the extreme northwest corner of the state.

This 56-mile route easily can be handled in a day with enough time left for exploring historic Fort Pickens and the sights along the Gulf beaches.

To reach the starting point on Pensacola Beach, take the Pensacola Bay Bridge out of Pensacola to U.S. Highway 98 East in Gulf Breeze. Get in the right-hand lane for the road to Fort Pickens and Pensacola Beach. Cross the Sikes Bridge over Santa Rosa Sound (there's a small toll), and you'll be on County Road 399. There's a large public parking lot at the corner of C.R. 399 and Fort Pickens Road where you can leave your car.

The first leg of the route will take you to Fort Pickens. When you leave the parking lot, the Gulf will be on your left and Sabine Bay on your right. There's a bike path shortly after you begin your ride. Though traffic isn't usually heavy, you might want to try the path. It extends for about 2.5 miles to the start of the Gulf Islands National Seashore. The park's entrance fee for bicycles is $1.

About eight miles into the ride there is a campground store, open from March to December.

The Visitor Information Center for Fort Pickens is less than three miles later. Give yourself at least an hour to tour the fort. Built from 1829 to 1834 by the U.S. Army Corps of Engineers with slave labor, the fort originally was designed to fortify Pensacola Harbor as the site of the principal Navy depot on the Gulf. It's built of massed earth and masonry, and 21.5 million bricks were used.

Fort Pickens

Most were purchased locally and brought to the island by barge.

The fort protected Pensacola Harbor during the Civil War and served as a prison for the Apache Indian chief Geronimo and 14 of his men from 1886 to 1888.

There is an impressive series of concrete batteries around the fort, and you can visit them on your bike. One of these was built during World War II after the sweeping victories by the Germans. Though the United States had not entered the war, the War Department chose to prepare a master plan for coastal defenses. The plan included two new 6-inch gun batteries.

The fort is open daily from 8:30 a.m. to 4 p.m., and guided tours are conducted Monday through Friday at 2 p.m. and on Saturday and Sunday at 11 a.m. and 2 p.m. A museum at the fort is open from 9 a.m. to 4 p.m. and offers interesting exhibits on natural and cultural history. A program also is offered daily at 3:30 p.m. in the auditorium.

A short distance from the fort is a 200-site campground, some sites with electrical hookups. Swimming in the Gulf is permitted, and there are lifeguards on duty. Outdoor showers also are available. The rangers at the fort can recommend good scuba diving areas.

On your return trip to the parking lot you'll visit the Dune Nature Trail, a good place to stop for a short hike. The dunes protect all these low-lying barrier islands that stretch for 150 miles from West Ship Island in Mississippi to the far end of Santa Rosa Island.

The beaches along here and in the Panhandle are the most magnificent in the state. The white sand stretches for miles, and the clear blue waters of the Gulf make these wide beaches an ideal place to spend a few hours, a few days or a few weeks.

Don't spend the entire 56 miles of this route on your bicycle; park long enough to admire the great scenery.

When you return to the parking lot, you'll have completed 20 miles of the route. There are good eating places nearby and stores offering cold drinks and snacks. Now you'll head in the opposite direction, covering about seven miles before re-entering the Gulf Islands National Seashore.

After about four miles, there's a public beach with restrooms, showers and a snack bar. This is an ideal place for swimming.

From there you have another three miles before you reach Navarre Beach. There's a long stretch here of beach cottages, apartment buildings and various commercial developments. *Jaws II* was filmed here.

It's about four more miles to the end of the road. There's a small grocery store and restrooms.

On the return journey, there are a few detours suggested that will take you off the main road. While traffic is rarely heavy, these detours will give you a little change of scenery and a look at some residential areas of Santa Rosa Island.

Shortly before the ride's end you'll have a bicycle path for about 2.5 miles. It parallels the main road, but it gets rough before the finish. You might want to return to Via de Luna for the last mile.

Santa Rosa Island is a long and very narrow strip of land. There are no trees and very little vegetation, so be prepared for a landscape that consists almost entirely of sand. The beaches are snow-white and they throw off a terrific glare. Wear sunglasses; the sun shines here about 300 days of the year.

For those coming here from other parts of Florida, Interstate 10 is the quickest route to Pensacola. From there the route to the beaches is well-marked.

This is a route that offers spectacular views of the Gulf, a chance to tour one of the oldest forts in the United States and wide, white beaches. Any tour of Florida would be incomplete without this one.

Fort Pickens-Navarre Beach loop

1. Turn left out of parking lot at corner of Via de Luna (C.R. 399) and Fort Pickens Road and go 9.5 miles to Visitor Information Center at Fort Pickens.
2. Turn left on returning to route after touring fort and go one-half mile to one-way sign.
3. Turn right at one-way sign and go seven-tenths of a mile to original route (C.R. 399).
4. Turn right on original route and go six-tenths of a mile to Dune Nature Trail.
5. Turn right on Dune Nature Trail and go four-tenths of a mile to Langdon Beach.
6. Turn right on original route and go 7.6 miles to parking lot.

7. Turn right out of parking lot onto Via de Luna and go seven-tenths of a mile to Avenida 10.
8. Turn right on Avenida 10 and go one-tenth of a mile to Ariola.
9. Turn left on Ariola and go 2.1 miles to Avenida 23.
10. Turn left on Avenida 23 and go one-tenth of a mile to Via de Luna.
11. Turn right on Via de Luna and go 4 miles to Gulf Islands National Seashore.
12. Enter Gulf Islands National Seashore and go 4.8 miles to public beach.
13. Return to C.R. 399 from public beach and go 2.7 miles to Navarre Beach.
14. Continue on Via de Luna for 3.7 miles to stop sign and enter parking lot.
15. Return to Via de Luna from parking lot and turn left. Go 1.2 miles to Arkansas Street, just past Tom Thumb-Citgo store.
16. Turn right on Arkansas Street and go one-tenth of a mile to White Sands Boulevard (first road on left).
17. Turn left on White Sands Boulevard and go 2 miles to South Carolina Street.
18. Turn left on South Carolina Street and go one-tenth of a mile to Gulf Boulevard.
19. Turn right on Gulf Boulevard and go 10.8 miles to Avenida de Manana, first road on right after Navarre private road.
20. Turn right on Avenida de Manana and go three-tenths of a mile to Michael Keenan Memorial Bicycle Path alongside Via de Luna.
21. Turn right on bicycle path and go 2.4 miles to Via de Luna.
22. Turn right on Via de Luna and go eight-tenths of a mile back to parking lot and end of route.

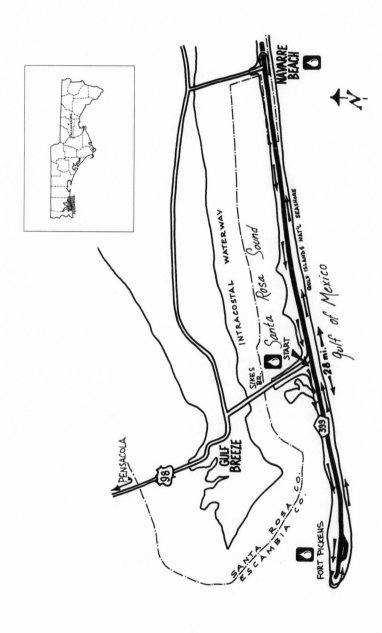

▲ Marianna-Sneads loop

One of the Panhandle's most scenic rides starts in Marianna, covers 85 miles and passes within a short distance of both Alabama and Georgia.

There are enough hills to make it interesting, miles of farmland and thick forests as you pedal through Jackson and Calhoun counties.

Jackson is the only Florida county bordering both Alabama and Georgia; you'll pass within two miles of Alabama at one point. Later you'll pedal south near the Chattahoochee River, sometimes close enough to see Georgia on the other bank.

You can pedal this route in one day, but many will want to break it into two days and spend a night at Three Rivers State Park. The distance is 45 miles on the first day; 40 miles on day No. 2.

Incorporated in 1828, Marianna, Jackson County's seat, is one of the oldest towns in the state. It has had a colorful history. The town, with a population of 7,000, has a variety of thriving industries.

Begin your ride at the public parking lot at the corner of Jackson and Madison streets behind the courthouse. Leave your car in that lot and notify the dispatcher in the nearby county jail that it's there. From there, pedal one block to U.S. Highway 90, then head north after another block on County Road 166.

Within three miles you'll be at Florida Caverns State Park. If you're making this a two-day ride, you will have plenty of time to sightsee. An intriguing network of caves lies below the 1,783 acres of the park. Though they're on a smaller scale than Mammoth Cave and Carlsbad Caverns, they equal those places in beauty.

The largest and most impressive is lighted and open

Florida Caverns State Park

to the public for ranger-guided tours.

The caverns were known to the Indians long before the white man arrived in this area. They are thought to have used the caves as a refuge from Gen. Andrew Jackson's forces during his expeditions into Spanish Florida in 1818.

After you've toured the caverns, an extensive trail system is available in the park. It meanders along the Chipola River through old growth, hardwood hammocks and limestone outcroppings. There are large stands of American beech, Southern magnolia, white oak and dogwood along the trail.

There are camping facilities in the park. You might want to begin your tour here, rather than at the courthouse in Marianna.

Your first turn off C.R. 166 is just three-tenths of a mile after leaving the park. There's no sign to indicate the turn onto C.R. 167, but it will be the first road on your left. From here to State Road 2 the surface sometimes is rough, and some of it is slag construction. The traffic is light and stays that way on the more than 13 miles of S.R. 2.

Much of the route is through rolling terrain past extensive farmland. The major crop in this area is peanuts, and Jackson County raises 82 per cent of all peanuts produced in Florida. Corn and soybeans account for the area's other chief products.

After leaving Marianna and before reaching Three Rivers State Park, there will be only one town along the route. That's Malone, a town with about 700 citizens. It is best known for producing a long succession of state high school championship basketball teams.

Heading south on C.R. 271, you'll be riding along the Chattahoochee River, which serves as a border between Georgia and Florida. The terrain gets hillier there, and it will stay that way all the way to the Three Rivers State Park.

The park is named for the Chattahoochee and Flint rivers, which merge to form the Apalachicola River below Lake Seminole. There are 682 hilly, heavily wooded acres in the park. Lake Seminole is man-made and was formed by flooding a large river swamp when the Jim Woodruff Dam was built in 1956 for the production of hydroelectricity.

Three Rivers is a great escape from the rat race. It's quiet and peaceful. White-tailed deer, gray fox, fox squirrel and other animals roam the woods, and alligators as well as huge alligator snapping turtles are common in the lake.

The picnic area and campground overlook Lake Seminole. There are restroom and shower facilities.

It's only two miles to Sneads and U.S. Highway 90 after you return to C.R. 271 the next morning. Sneads has about 1,600 people, and it's the nearest spot for supplies if you need any for your stay in the park.

Watch closely for C.R. 286 that you take out of Sneads. The road is not well-marked, but you should have no trouble if you follow directions.

When you get on C.R. 286, you'll encounter a long curve in the road at the eight-mile mark just after crossing into Calhoun County. After crossing S.R. 69, C.R. 286 becomes C.R 274. It will be about seven more miles to Altha, a town with about 450 people. This will be the last town on the route before returning to Marianna. In Altha you'll turn onto S.R. 71 and pedal for about 11 miles before turning left on C.R. 280. Take the second road that's marked C.R. 280, not the first.

After three miles on C.R. 280, turn onto S.R. 73 which takes you back to Jackson Street in Marianna behind the courthouse. It's just one block from there to the end of the route.

For those who like to crowd a lot of miles into every day of touring, you'll have no trouble doing this route in a single day. But with two very attractive state parks along the way you won't have time to loiter long in either of them.

This route is good for riding at any time of the year, but those who opt to camp at Three Rivers in the winter months better have a good sleeping bag. The nights next to the Georgia and Alabama border can be chilly. The days, though, are ideal.

Marianna-Sneads loop

1. Turn right out of parking lot onto Madison Street and go one block to U.S. Highway 90.
2. Turn left on U.S. Highway 90 and go one-tenth of a mile to C.R. 166.
3. Turn right on C.R. 166 and go 2.8 miles to Florida Caverns State Park.
4. Turn left out of state park on C.R. 166 and go three-tenths of a mile to C.R. 167.
5. Turn left on C.R. 167 and go 10.7 miles to S.R. 2.
6. Turn right on S.R. 2 and go 13.4 miles to C.R. 164.
7. Turn right on C.R. 164 and go 1.3 miles to C.R. 271.
8. Turn left on C.R. 271 and go 16.7 miles to Three Rivers State Park.
9. Turn left after leaving Three Rivers State Park and go 2.1 miles to U.S. Highway 90 in Sneads.
10. Cross U.S. Highway 90 and go one block to Old Spanish Trail.
11. Turn left on Old Spanish Trail and go one-half of a mile to C.R. 286 (Gloster Avenue). Abandoned building is on right.

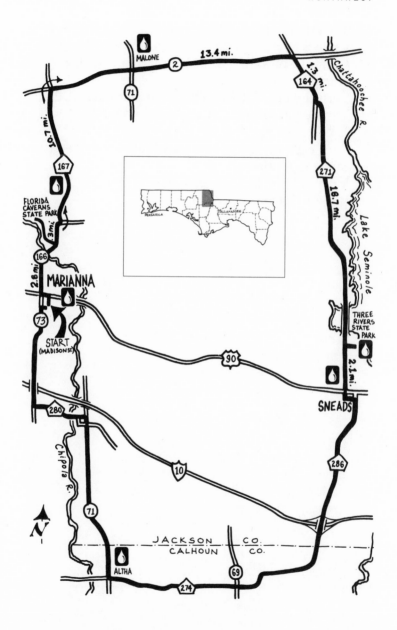

12. Turn right on C.R. 286 and go 13.1 miles to S.R. 69.
13. Cross S.R. 69; C.R. 286 becomes C.R. 274.
14. Continue on C.R. 274 for 6.7 miles to S.R. 71 in Altha.
15. Turn right on S.R. 71 and go 10.8 miles to C.R. 280.
16. Turn left at second C.R. 280 sign and go 3 miles to S.R. 73.
17. Turn right on S.R. 73 and go 3.4 miles to Jackson Street in Marianna.
18. Turn right on Jackson Street and go one block to parking lot and end of route.

▲ Milton-Chumuckla loop

This 70-mile loop begins and ends in Milton in Florida's extreme northwest. Its meandering route through Santa Rosa County takes you within about six miles of the Alabama border. Only neighboring Escambia County (Pensacola) is further west.

Like most other counties in the Panhandle, Santa Rosa has varied terrain. From sea level in the southern part on the Gulf of Mexico, the elevation climbs to 280 feet. Much of this route will be in the higher elevations — rolling country that will give you a chance to shift gears.

From Milton the route heads immediately north, and the only traffic you'll encounter in this sparsely populated area is when you leave and then re-enter Milton. The roads through this wooded countryside are good.

Before leaving Milton, browse through the historic district downtown. It's right next to the public parking lot, catty-cornered from the Santa Rosa County Courthouse at the corner of Elmira Street and U.S. Highway 90. The restored Imogene Theatre has become a local showplace, as have the many beautiful old homes.

Less than two miles from the starting point you'll be in the rural areas along County Road 191. The Navy's Whiting Field, used for training helicopter pilots, is about seven miles from Milton, just off C.R. 191.

Much of the area along C.R. 191 is wooded, but the trees get thicker as you enter the Blackwater River State Forest. You'll be on C.R. 191 for almost 20 miles before turning west onto State Road 4 in Munson.

There are some good hills before you reach Munson and more after you leave town. When you leave S.R. 4 and head south you'll ride through densely wooded areas occasionally dotted by small farms. One of the prettiest stretches of the route will be the 3.4 miles on Cobbtown Road. This beautiful road winds through the woods, and it's quite likely you won't see any traffic.

Watch closely for Cobbtown Road. It's not well-marked, but there are two churches at the corner where you make the turn from C.R. 164.

Stores on this route are few and far between. There's one in Munson and not another until you reach Chumuckla on C.R. 197.

From Chumuckla, the rest of the ride , about 20 miles, will be on gently rolling terrain. The traffic is light until you reach the outskirts of Milton on C.R. 191. From there it's only a few more miles to the parking lot as you retrace some of the same roads you took at the ride's beginning.

From Milton, it's only two miles to Bagdad. County Road 191 is a short distance from the parking lot; it leads back to Interstate 10. Turn on C.R. 191 and it will take you right into Bagdad.

Bagdad had dozens of lumber mills during its boom days in the 1820s until the 1930s, but the last mill closed in 1937. A long period of decline followed until the local historical society became active in restoration. Now it's a quaint historic village with dozens of restored Victorian houses. While you're in the town, make sure to visit the old L&N depot, which also has been restored. It's now a museum of local history and an art gallery.

This route is one of two in this same area of the Panhandle. You might want to make a weekend of biking by riding the route on Santa Rosa Island that includes visits to Fort Pickens and Navarre Beach. That's a 56-mile route, an easy day's ride.

For those who plan to travel both routes on a weekend, there are lots of places to stay. There are good

Blackwater River State Park

campgrounds in the area.

If you prefer tent camping, your best bet is Blackwater River State Park. The Blackwater River flows right through Milton; the park is located in the Blackwater River State Forest northeast of Milton.

After you've finished the ride out of Milton, return to C.R 191 and head a few miles north until you reach the road that turns east toward the state park. The crystal-clear river and beautiful white sand beaches make it ideal for swimming. There are restrooms, hot showers and well-equipped picnic areas. The thickly wooded park is very well-maintained.

Santa Rosa County has become one of Florida's more prosperous areas. In addition to its proximity to three major air bases, oil was discovered in Jay, a few miles off your route, in the early 1970s. Now the farm fields are dotted with oil wells. More than 5 million barrels of oil are produced in the county each year.

Crop farming is still big, despite the appearance of oil

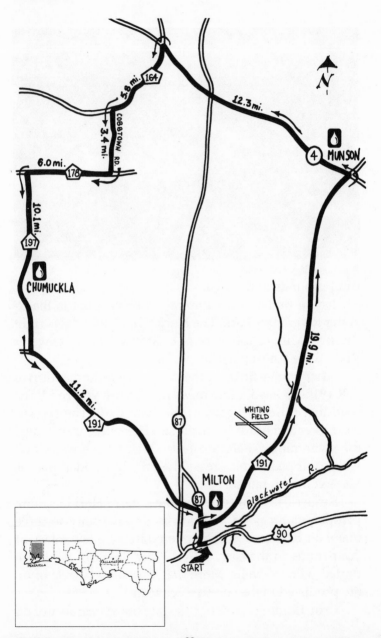

on the scene, and Santa Rosa is the top cotton-producing county in the state. Other major crops include potatoes, cabbage and pecans.

A two-day tour of this part of the state will let you enjoy a marked contrast in scenery — hills and woods north of Milton, sandy beaches and dunes later.

The Panhandle is vastly different from the rest of the state — it's not even in the same time zone!

Milton-Chumuckla loop

1. Turn right out of parking lot onto U.S. Highway 90 and go three-tenths of a mile to S.R. 87.
2. Turn right on S.R. 87 and go eight-tenths of a mile to C.R. 191.
3. Turn right on C.R. 191 and go 19.9 miles to S.R. 4.
4. Turn left on S.R. 4 and go 12.3 miles to C.R. 164.
5. Turn left on C.R. 164 and go 5.8 miles to Cobbtown Road. Cobbtown Holiness Church and Cobbtown Mennonite Church are at this corner.
6. Turn left on Cobbtown Road and go 3.4 miles to C.R. 178.
7. Turn right on C.R. 178 and go 6 miles to C.R. 197.
8. Turn left on C.R. 197 and go 10.1 miles to C.R. 191.
9. Turn left on C.R. 191 and go 11.2 miles to S.R. 87.
10. Turn right on S.R. 87 and go 1.6 miles to U.S. Highway 90.
11. Turn left on U.S. Highway 90 and go three-tenths of a mile to parking lot and end of route.

▲ Wewahitchka-Mexico Beach loop

A route that begins and ends in a town with the unusual name of Wewahitchka will take you through nearly 70 miles of Gulf and Bay counties and expose you to a lot of wilderness, a long stretch along the Gulf of Mexico, a suburb of the second largest city in the Panhandle and a major U.S. Air Force base.

Because there's heavy traffic at times on U.S. Highway 98 between late May and Labor Day, you might want to take this trip during another time of year. The rest of the route is on roads that are always quiet.

The terrain throughout the ride is flat, but the scenery offers some decided changes. The roads are good.

Wewahitchka was the county seat of Gulf County until 1964, when voters decided to move it to Port St. Joe. It's a quiet place with about 1,800 people, on the shores of Dead Lake. This 80-square-mile lake has some of the best freshwater fishing in the United States. It was formed many years ago when the waters of the Apalachicola and Chipola rivers converged during a flood and filled a cypress swamp.

The old courthouse, now being used by the Department of Health and Rehabilitative Services, is still there, and your starting point at City Hall is just two blocks away.

You can park your car behind the City Hall, pedal one block to Main Street (State Road 71) and be on your way.

You'll be on County Road 386 for almost 20 miles through country that's mostly wilderness. Much of it is swampy, and the traffic is very light.

You'll be in the resort town of Mexico Beach on the Gulf at the end of that stretch. You might want to stop and relax there. The Panhandle is famous for its white-sand beaches. The beach stretches for miles and is a great place to enjoy a swim and work on your tan before riding the last 50 miles back to Wewahitchka. You'll have no trouble finding places for a cold drink and snack or a meal.

For the next three miles you'll ride through businesses and developments aimed at tourists. From Mexico Beach to Panama City Beach there are many more miles of the same.

Mexico Beach is about 30 miles east of Panama City and is the eastern terminus of what is referred to as the Miracle Strip. Because of its proximity to Tyndall Air Force Base, most of the people enjoying Mexico Beach are service personnel and their families. Few tourists find their way below Tyndall to Mexico Beach.

It's much quieter in Mexico Beach than in Panama City Beach, where it can get pretty wild as the mobs descend on the place during the summer.

This part of Florida is nicknamed the Redneck Riviera because it attracts thousands of tourists from other Southern states. During the summer as you get closer to Panama City, traffic on U.S. Highway 98 is gridlocked.

Shortly after leaving Mexico Beach you'll reach Tyndall Air Force Base. You'll ride along the border of this installation for more than 10 miles before you reach the base's main gate at the 37-mile mark. From here the road becomes a divided, four-lane highway for the next seven miles.

You'll ride through the town of Callaway, a suburb of Panama City, before turning onto C.R. 22. This is generally referred to as Wewa Highway, and you'll ride on it for the 25 miles back to the starting point.

The last miles are through the Gaskin Wildlife Management area, and it's pine forests most of the way.

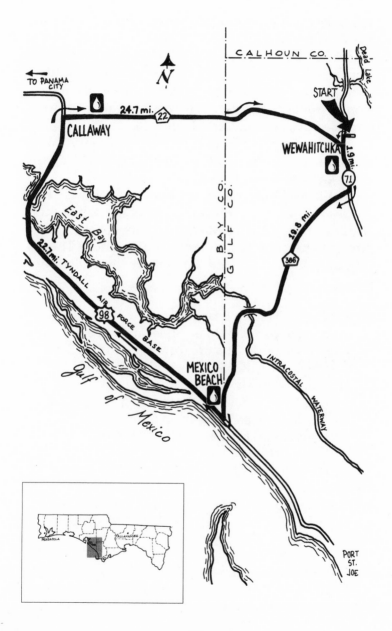

The timber is processed at big paper mills in Port St. Joe and Panama City.

Wewahitchka, founded in 1875, is a Seminole Indian word meaning "watery eyes". Many of the early settlers were Confederate veterans seeking a new life on the Florida frontier after the Civil War. Most of them were from Georgia, Alabama and Tennessee.

Besides the paper industry, Wewahitchka is probably best known for the Tupelo honey it produces. It bills itself as the Land of Honey.

You'll enjoy this route with its sharp contrasts from a sleepy town like Wewahitchka to the white-sand beaches of the Gulf of Mexico and its developments, through the pine woods and swamplands. There's enough to hold your interest and make for a full day of biking.

Wewahitchka-Mexico Beach loop

1. Turn left at corner of Main Street and Osceola Avenue onto S.R. 71 and go 1.9 miles to C.R. 386.
2. Turn right on C.R. 386 and go 19.8 miles to U.S. Highway 98 in Mexico Beach.
3. Turn right on U.S. Highway 98 and go 22.7 miles to C.R. 22 (Wewa Highway) in Callaway.
4. Turn right on C.R. 22 and go 24.7 miles to S.R. 71 in Wewahitchka.
5. Turn left on S.R. 71 and go one-tenth of a mile to Osceola Avenue.
6. Turn right on Osceola Avenue and go one block to parking lot behind City Hall and end of route.

▲Wewahitchka-Port St. Joe loop

This route from Wewahitchka to the Gulf of Mexico via the busy paper-producing town of Port St. Joe lets you explore one of the most scenic stretches of unspoiled beaches and dunes along the Gulf coast.

This route is about 42 miles from Wewahitchka to your destination at St. Joseph Peninsula State Park, and the return trip is over the same roads. Though the 84-mile round trip easily can be ridden in one day, it is suggested you take two days and spend the night at the park.

This route is entirely in Gulf County, a county that wasn't established until 1925 but one with an extensive history. The town of Port St. Joe has been around since 1835, and the Spanish had an outpost on St. Joseph Bay as early as 1701.

Gulf County is best known for paper production. The St. Joe Paper Company opened in 1938, and other major industries have followed to make Port St. Joe the third-largest chemical-producing town in Florida.

With so much paper production, it is not surprising that there are thousands of acres of forest in the county. Shortly after you begin the ride in Wewahitchka on S.R. 71, you'll be immersed in thick woods.

Plan to leave your car behind the City Hall in Wewahitchka and go one block on Osceola Avenue to Main Street, State Road 71.

You'll pedal through pine woods for 24 miles between Wewahitchka and Port St. Joe. The traffic on this road is light, and the terrain is flat enough that approaching traffic has plenty of time to spot bicyclists.

White City is about 17 miles into the trip. You can buy cold drinks at the store there, and just after that you'll cross the bridge over the Intracoastal Waterway. This waterway is the dividing line between the Central and Eastern time zones; some residents of the county are an hour ahead of others.

Port St. Joe is a bustling community with about 5,000 people, and many of the residents work at the nearby industrial plants.

Just after you turn onto U.S. Highway 19-98 in Port St. Joe, you'll pass a state historic site that's worth stopping to see. Florida's first constitution was written by the territorial convention that met here in December 1838. An imposing monument commemorating this event and a museum have been erected there by the state. The museum has interesting exhibits about the convention and the constitution it prepared. It's open daily except Tuesday and Wednesday. Picnic facilities make it an excellent spot to stop for lunch.

After a visit to the monument and museum, you'll return to U.S. Highway 19-98 briefly before switching to S.R. 30 for several miles. State Road 30 turns onto S.R. 30E, which takes you into the state park.

Because of its remote location, St. Joseph Peninsula State Park is little known to most Florida residents and is seldom crowded. The long, narrow peninsula it is situated on has the Gulf on one side and St. Joseph Bay on the other. When you reach the park you're nearly opposite the town of Port St. Joe on the other side of St. Joseph Bay.

The white sand beaches and large dunes stretch for miles along the Gulf in the park, which has 2,516 acres and excellent facilities. There's a large area for tent camping with showers and restrooms. There are eight cabins in another part of the park that can be rented for a minimum of two nights in the off-season from September through February and a minimum of five nights during

St. Joseph Peninsula State Park

the busier summer months.

Reservations for the cabins will be accepted only by telephone or in person. Reservations for camping will be accepted only by telephone; (904) 227-1327.

Most of the park's interior is heavily wooded and it has become an outstanding bird-watching area. There have been 209 species of birds sighted in the park. Shore birds and wading birds are particularly numerous.

In St. Joseph Bay, the water is quite shallow and it teems with marine life, including bay scallops, hermit crabs, fiddler crabs, horseshoe crabs and octopuses.

If you don't want to camp in the park, but you would like to spend the day, there are motels in Port St. Joe. The ride there from the park is about 18 miles.

The park's beaches are superb for swimming or just for strolling and shelling if you're visiting in the winter. There are boardwalks leading to the beaches to prevent destruction of the protective dunes.

An 11,650-acre wilderness preserve stretching for five miles is on the northern part of the park. Bird watching is a favorite pastime here, and a bird list is available at the park office. There are hiking routes along the peninsula's center and the bay and beach shores.

Despite the many nearby industrial plants, visitors to the St. Joseph Peninsula State Park with its miles of unspoiled white sand beaches feel as if they are hundreds of miles from civilization. It's a quiet place and a great spot to stop and relax after 42 miles of pedaling through the pine woods and along the shores of St. Joseph Bay.

In recent years, mostly during the '80s, many people have discovered the area leading to the state park and have built vacation homes, condos and town houses along the Gulf and the bay. The park remains untouched by all this development.

After spending the night at the park or in Port St. Joe, the ride back over the same roads to Wewahitchka and your starting point will be easy.

Wewahitchka-Port St. Joe loop
1. Turn left at corner of Main Street and Osceola Avenue onto S.R. 71 and go 24.5 miles to U.S. Highway 19-98 in Port St. Joe.
2. Turn left on U.S. Highway 19-98 and go 1.2 miles to road turning into the Constitution Museum.
3. Return from museum, turn left on U.S. Highway 19-98 and go seven-tenths of a mile to S.R. 30.
4. Turn right on S.R. 30 and go 6.9 miles to S.R. 30E, leading into St. Joseph Peninsula State Park.
5. Turn right on S.R. 30E into park and go 8.8 miles to park entrance.
6. Return to S.R. 30 on S.R. 30E.
7. Turn left on S.R. 30 and go 6.9 miles to U.S. Highway 19-98.
8. Turn left on U.S. Highway 98 and go 1.9 miles to S.R. 71.

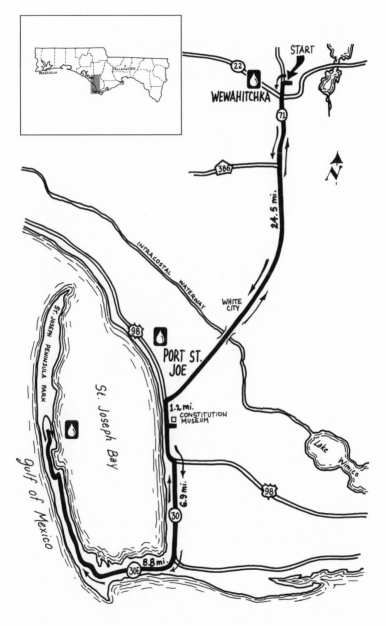

START

WEWAHITCHKA

22

71

386

24.5 mi.

WHITE CITY

INTRACOSTAL WATERWAY

ST. JOSEPH PENINSULA PARK

St. Joseph Bay

98

PORT ST. JOE

1.2 mi.
CONSTITUTION MUSEUM

Gulf of Mexico

6.9 mi.

30

98

Lake Wimico

8.8 mi.

30E

PENSACOLA

TALLAHASSEE

N

9. Turn right on S.R. 71 and go 24.5 miles to starting point at the corner of Main Street and Osceola Avenue in Wewahitchka.

▲ *Madison-Monticello loop*

Monticello and Madison are two of the nicest towns in North Florida, making this ride between them a real delight. You might want to break this 87-mile trip into two days and spend some time looking around.

It's 50 miles from Madison to Monticello which would leave 37 miles for the second day.

You'll ride on quiet roads through gently rolling terrain for most of the trip, and though you'll be on U.S. Highway 90 for more than 16 miles on your return, you won't experience traffic problems. Interstate 10 runs parallel to U.S. Highway 90 between the towns; there's only local traffic on U.S. Highway 90.

Park your car near the courthouse in the center of Madison. It's on U.S. Highway 90. There's a city park across the street with a Confederate monument and another memorial honoring Colin Kelly, a Madison native who was the nation's first Medal of Honor winner during World War II.

Turn north on State Road 53 from U.S. Highway 90. The Wardlaw-Smith mansion is on your left. It was built in 1860 and used as a hospital for Confederate soldiers injured in the Battle of Olustee during the Civil War.

There's very little traffic on S.R. 53, and you'll enjoy the scenic countryside with its neat farms and homes.

After you leave S.R. 53 and turn onto C.R. 150, there's a junction that could cause some confusion. After nearly seven miles you'll come to the junction of C.R. 150 and C.R. 146. Veer right on C.R. 146 and go less than a mile to where you make a left turn and return to C.R. 150 heading south.

The route takes you onto U.S. Highway 221 for about eight miles, but traffic here also is light.

You will enter Monticello on C.R. 146 and go several blocks through the residential areas before turning onto U.S. Highway 90. This will take you to the Jefferson County Courthouse in the center of Monticello. Both U.S. Highway 19 and U.S. Highway 90 converge on Monticello at the courthouse, and both highways circle the building. When you get to the courthouse look for the sign indicating U.S. Highway 90 East. That road will take you back to Madison.

Before starting your return trip, take some time to look around Monticello. The chamber of commerce will give you a brochure that will guide you on a walking tour of this fascinating town. You'll see antebellum homes, a restored opera house that was built in 1890 and a courthouse that was patterned after Thomas Jefferson's home in Virginia.

If you're planning to make this loop a two-day ride, there are motels and restaurants in Monticello.

About 9.5 miles into the second day's ride on U.S. Highway 90 near the Aucilla River, there's a historic marker telling about the DeSoto Trail. Hernando De Soto's expedition crossed the flooded Aucilla River in October 1539. The river was 200 yards wide instead of the normal 10 to 15 yards, and De Soto and his party, besieged by Indians, finally crossed the river in two and a half days.

After passing through Greenville, your route turns south on U.S. Highway 221. After you cross Interstate 10 but before you get into Madison, you'll come to the junction of C.R. 360A and C.R. 14. You will have been on C.R. 14. When C.R. 14 veers right, you continue straight ahead on C.R. 360A. This road will take you back to Madison via U.S. Highway 90, where you make a right turn and ride a half-mile to the courthouse and the end of the route.

Madison County is primarily an agricultural county with cotton, pecans, corn, tobacco and watermelon as the major crops. You will be riding past many farms producing these crops.

Established in 1827, Madison is one of Florida's older counties. You will want to tour the town with its well-preserved antebellum homes dating to 1849.

A restoration project is planned to make the downtown area appear as it did in 1914.

Though some cotton still is grown in Madison County, cotton no longer is king as it was in the last century. More than 200,000 acres of sea-island cotton were being raised in Florida by the 1870s, and Madison was one of the centers of the industry. A reminder of those years is in a park near the railroad, where a 16-foot drive wheel for a 500-horsepower engine that pulled 65 gins in the world's largest cotton processing plant is resting beside a small patch of cotton.

Tobacco now is the county's No. 1 crop. It's the flue-cured tobacco that's used in making cigarettes.

It's easy to spend half a day browsing around Madison just as it was in Monticello. That's why this ride is suggested as a two-day trip.

For those planning to spend the night in Madison, there are motels and restaurants. There is also a good campground on S.R. 53.

Be sure to fill your water bottles before leaving on this trip. There's no town between Madison and Monticello on the first day, and only Greenville on the 37-mile return trip.

Madison-Monticello loop
1. Turn left on U.S. Highway 90 at Range Street next to courthouse and go one-tenth of a mile to S.R. 53.

2. Turn right on S.R. 53 and go 8.1 miles to C.R. 150.
3. Turn left on C.R. 150 and go 6.8 miles to junction of C.R. 146 and C.R. 150.
4. Veer right on C.R. 146 for seven-tenths of a mile to C.R. 150.
5. Turn left on C.R. 150 and go 7.8 miles to C.R. 140.
6. Turn right on C.R. 140 and go 2.8 miles to U.S. Highway 221.
7. Turn right on U.S. Highway 221 and go 8.1 miles to C.R. 146.
8. Turn left on C.R. 146 and go 14.7 miles to Monticello, disregarding C.R. 146 sign in town.
9. Continue on C.R. 146 to four-way stop in Monticello. Monticello Auto Towing is on left.
10. Turn left at four-way stop and go one-tenth of a mile to U.S. Highway 90.
11. Turn right on U.S. Highway 90 and go three-tenths of a mile to circular road around courthouse to U.S. Highway 90 East.
12. Go straight ahead on U.S. Highway 90 East for 16.2 miles to U.S. Highway 221 in town of Greenville.
13. Turn right on U.S. Highway 221 and go 3.2 miles to C.R. 158.
14. Turn left on C.R. 158 and go 10.2 miles to C.R. 14.
15. Turn left on C.R. 14 and go 3.6 miles, across Interstate 10 to C.R. 360A.
16. Go straight on C.R. 360A. C.R. 14 goes right there. Stay on C.R. 360A for 3.6 miles to U.S. Highway 90 in Madison.
17. Turn right on U.S. Highway 90 and go one-half of a mile to Range Street.
18. Turn right on Range Street and return to parking area for end of route.

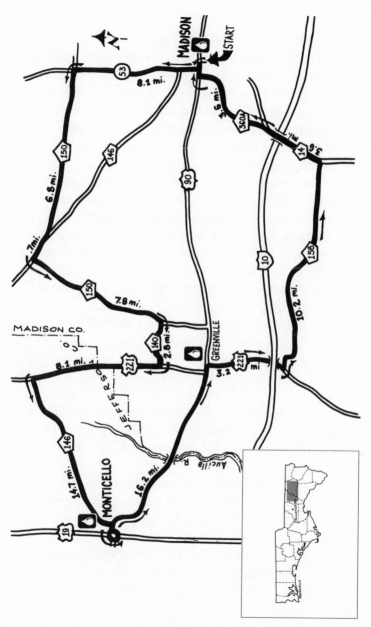

39

▲ Monticello-Leon County loop

Some of Florida's hilliest country surrounds Tallahassee, the state capital. This 52-mile loop from Monticello west to Leon County leads you through rolling country and gives you plenty of time to browse around Monticello, one of Florida's prettiest small towns.

Begin your ride at the courthouse in the center of Monticello, Jefferson County's seat. You'll have no trouble finding it. Built in 1909, this silver-domed courthouse is at the intersection of two U.S. highways. U.S. Highway 19 goes north and south through Monticello, and drivers have to take a circular road around the courthouse. Those approaching from the east or west on U.S. Highway 90 also must drive that same circular road. It almost makes the courthouse look as if it's sitting in the middle of a merry-go-round.

The town's business district is a short distance from the courthouse, so you'll have no trouble finding a spot to park your car. Despite the two U.S. highways going through the center of the town, Monticello is a quiet place.

It's 25 miles to Tallahassee from Monticello, and some residents commute to jobs at the capital or Florida State University. All but 10 miles of this loop are in Jefferson County.

As you head south, there will be some hills before you turn off U.S. Highway 19 onto County Road 259. Nearly half of the trip will be spent on this road that eventually will take you into Leon County. You'll cross U.S. Highway 27 and C.R. 59 before leaving Jefferson County. The terrain is somewhat rolling, but it's not challenging. The area is sparsely populated, and much of it is wooded.

When you get to Leon County, about 22 miles from the starting point, you'll still be on C.R. 259, though its name later changes to Tram Road. It's mostly wilderness on the outskirts of Florida's capital. Traffic is light.

From C.R. 259 you'll head north on W.W. Kelley Road before reaching U.S. Highway 27 for your return to Jefferson County.

There will be no problem on U.S. Highway 27. It's a divided four-lane highway, and the traffic is light for the 6.3 miles you're riding on it.

The only problem you'll experience with signs will be after leaving U.S. Highway 27 heading down C.R. 59. At the five-mile mark on this road, you're supposed to turn right onto C.R. 158A. There's no sign there; remember to turn right at the Phillips 66 gas station on your left.

The only traffic you may encounter will be on the 2.3 miles of U.S. Highway 90 that take you back to the Monticello courthouse. You will be just a mile from the Monticello city limits when you get on this two-lane road.

Even slow riders should be able to negotiate this route in little more than four hours. You'll have plenty of time to explore Monticello.

The town, then called Jefferson Courthouse, was founded in 1826. When Jefferson died later that year, it was renamed Monticello, after the third president's home. In 1827, Jefferson County was founded.

Monticello's courthouse was built on the site of the county's original courthouse. Patterned after Jefferson's home, it cost $40,000 to build, and it has become the town's centerpiece.

There's a lot to see, and the chamber of commerce distributes brochures for a self-guided walking tour of the town.

Across the street from the courthouse is Perkins

Opera House, built in 1890. It was restored to its original appearance in the late 1980s in time for its centennial. In its early days, the stage was the largest in the Southeast. There are 600 seats, and regular performances still are staged there, usually by touring groups that augment the cast with local talent.

Take a look around the opera house. The town has done a remarkable job of restoring a building that was almost ready for the wrecker's ball a few years ago.

There are more than 40 buildings from the 19th century still in use, and many of the homes are antebellum. The oldest is the Wirick-Simmons House, built in 1833. There are three churches with stained glass windows from the last century and a cemetery that dates back to 1827 with graves of people born in the 18th century and Confederate and Union soldiers.

Another highlight of the tour is the Avenue of Oaks, a cathedral of giant oaks planted in 1889.

Jefferson County has a population of only 10,000, and Monticello is the only incorporated town in the county. Pecans and watermelons are grown extensively in the county, and there also is timber and livestock.

This is a delightful route over quiet roads, through pleasant country with a beautiful Florida town as the starting and finishing point.

If you've set aside a full weekend for biking, there's another tour nearby that can be handled on the second day. That would be the route from Madison to Monticello, an 87-mile ride.

Monticello-Leon County loop

1. Go south on U.S. Highway 19 from courthouse for 1.6 miles to C.R. 259.

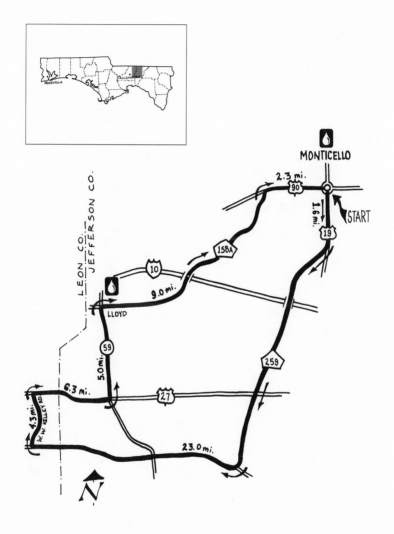

2. Turn right on C.R. 259 and go 23 miles to W. W. Kelley Road.
3. Turn right on W. W. Kelley Road and go 4.3 miles to U.S. Highway 27.
4. Turn right on U.S. Highway 27 and go 6.3 miles to C.R. 59.
5. Turn left on C.R. 59 and go 5 miles to C.R. 158A. It's unmarked, but there's a Phillips 66 gas station on the left.
6. Turn right on S.R. 158A and go 9 miles to U.S. Highway 90.
7. Turn right on U.S. Highway 90 and go 2.3 miles to courthouse in Monticello and end of route.

▲ Quincy-Torreya State Park loop

Bring along all your gears for this ride through Gadsden and Liberty counties in the Panhandle. This 113-mile route will prove that far from being only a vast expanse of flatlands, Florida has some very challenging hills.

This ride is designed as a two-day trip with an overnight stop at Torreya State Park. The first day covers 73 miles, leaving 40 miles for the final day. The shorter second day gives you enough time to enjoy the park.

Quincy, about 20 miles west of Tallahassee, is the starting and finishing place for this loop. Police suggest that you park your car at the Dollar General Store across the street from city hall and the police station at the corner of Stewart and Jefferson streets. The area is well-lighted and regularly patrolled.

There are almost 30 changes of highways on this route, so you will have to pay close attention to the directions.

You will be in rural country in little more than a mile from the starting point, and the terrain will be hilly on State Road 65. There are several highway changes in the first 16 miles, but there are no problems until you reach S.R. 12.

As you ride down County Road 159, you'll see a sign that indicates the road turns left. Ignore this sign; cross S.R. 12, make a short jog to the right and continue straight ahead until you reach U.S. Highway 27.

There might be some confusion when you turn onto U.S. Highway 90. You travel for only one-tenth of a mile before you turn right on C.R. 268. There's a gas station and deli on the corner.

While you're in Gadsden County, the roads change

constantly. Pay close attention to the directions.

You'll start getting into hills when you enter Liberty County. About four miles before you reach Torreya State Park, you'll find a real monster. There's a long sweep down this hill, which should be enough to take you well up the other side. But long before reaching the top, you'll be shifting gears. It's best to go as low as possible because the climb is a tough one. And don't relax when you reach level ground at the top. More hills await you before you ride into Torreya.

You'll be on C.R. 270 during the climb. Parts of the highway are fairly rough, but the surface on the hills is not bad. The two miles before and after the park are rough, then there will be good roads the rest of the way.

Torreya is a peaceful and scenic park. It has full facilities. There are high bluffs facing the Apalachicola River in Torreya, some of them 150 feet above the river. Deep ravines have been etched into the bluffs by eroding streams.

Hardwood trees, commonly found in the Appalachian Mountains of North Georgia, are found on these bluffs and ravines. These hardwoods give the finest show of fall color in Florida, so keep this in mind and plan your ride for October or November.

The park is named after the rare Torreya tree that grows only on the bluffs along the Apalachicola River. It once was plentiful, but it was decimated by a blight that began in 1960 and may doom this species to extinction.

Torreya is rich in history. Archeologists have found evidence of ancient Indian settlements, and during the first Seminole Indian War in 1818, Gen. Andrew Jackson crossed the river here with his army.

After Florida became a U.S. territory, the first government road, built in 1828 across North Florida, led to the

The Gregory House at Torreya State Park

river at Torreya. The river was an important interstate link in the 1800s, and during the great trading era between 1840 and 1910 more than 200 steamboats were operating.

A particular point of interest in the park is the Gregory House. Built across the river at Ocheesee Landing in 1849 by planter Jason Gregory, the plantation prospered until the Civil War and the abolition of slavery. In 1935 the house was dismantled and moved to its present site by the Civilian Conservation Corps.

The area also figured in the Civil War. A battery of six cannons was manned on the bluff to prevent Union gunboats from passing. The gun pits still can be seen along the bluff trail.

There are several nature trails in the park, including the Apalachicola River Bluffs Trail and the National Recreation Trail that provide a view of the river, the

Confederate gun pits, the bluffs and hardwood forest. The Weeping Ridge Trail also features a nice walk to a deep ravine. Rangers give daily tours of the restored Gregory House.

Campfire programs are offered on Saturday nights in the camping area.

When you leave Torreya the next morning you won't have long to wait for more hills. There's another long, steep rise just after you enter Gadsden County on C.R. 270.

Only slightly more than 20 miles of this route are in Liberty County, and those are in the extreme northern corner. Liberty County, the second smallest county in the state, had a population of only 4,260 in the 1980 census. It has 837 square miles, which figures out to only 5.1 people per square mile and makes Liberty the most sparsely populated county in Florida. There's only one major crop in the county — timber. You'll see plenty of it as you pedal.

Your return to Gadsden County will come soon after leaving Torreya. Early in the second day you'll encounter a couple of confusing points. The first of these is less than two miles after leaving Torreya. That would be at the junction of C.R. 271 and C.R. 1641. The latter is on the left and is marked as the road to Bristol, the county seat of Liberty County. Don't take it but continue on C.R. 271 until you come to the junction with C.R. 270, where you make a sharp turn to the left.

A few miles after that junction you'll see a sign and arrow on your left pointing toward Chattahoochee. The road, C.R. 269, is on your left, but it's unmarked. Turn there. After 5.6 miles, make another turn onto C.R. 268 at Rosedale.

The route goes through Gretna, about 15 miles from

the loop's finish. There's a store there as well as another about four miles before reaching Gretna.

You'll ride about three miles on S.R. 65 — the same highway you rode on leaving Quincy — before you return to U.S. Highway 90 and the last few blocks back to the parking lot.

Quincy, the county seat of Gadsden County, has a population of about 8,500. Antebellum homes and old-fashioned gardens of jasmine, camellias and roses are the town's pride. The county is a major producer of tobacco, corn and peanuts. Gadsden County's average elevation is 260 feet, which makes it one of the highest counties in Florida.

The long hills on this route and the overnight stop at an outstanding state park make this an enjoyable trip.

Quincy-Torreya State Park loop

1. Turn right out of parking lot onto U.S. Highway 90 and go three-tenths of a mile to S.R. 65.
2. Turn left on S.R. 65 and go 3.5 miles to C.R. 270.
3. Turn right on C.R. 270 and go 4.1 miles to C.R. 161.
4. Turn left on C.R. 161 and go 3.4 miles to C.R. 159.
5. Turn right on C.R. 159 and go 5.4 miles to U.S. Highway 27.
6. Turn right on U.S. Highway 27 and go nine-tenths of a mile to C.R. 159.
7. Turn right on C.R. 159 and go 1.8 miles to C.R. 270.
8. Turn left on C.R. 270 and go two-tenths of a mile to C.R. 159.
9. Turn right on C.R. 159 and go 5.7 miles to U.S. Highway 90.
10. Turn left on U.S. Highway 90 and go one-tenth of a mile to C.R. 268.
11. Turn right on C.R. 268 and go 6.9 miles to C.R. 65B.

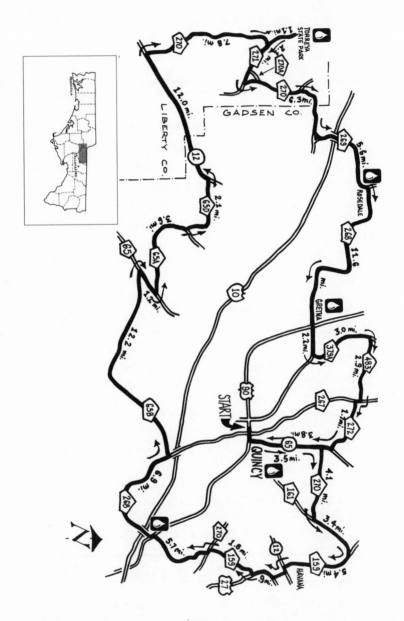

12. Turn left on C.R. 65B and go 12.2 miles to C.R. 65.

13. Turn right on C.R. 65 and go 1.2 miles to C.R. 65A.

14. Turn left on C.R. 65A and go 3.6 miles to C.R. 65D.

15. Turn left on C.R. 65D and go 2.1 miles to S.R. 12.

16. Turn left on S.R. 12 and go 12 miles to C.R. 270.

17. Turn right on C.R. 270 and go 7.8 miles to C.R. 271.

18. Turn left on C.R. 271 and go 1.1 miles to Torreya State Park.

19. Turn left on C.R. 271 upon leaving the park and go 2.1 miles to C.R. 270.

20. Turn left on C.R. 270 and go 6.3 miles to C.R. 269. No sign for road there but arrow and sign point toward Chattahoochee.

21. Turn left at sign pointing toward Chattahoochee and go 5.6 miles to C.R. 268 in Rosedale.

22. Turn right on C.R. 268 and go 11.6 miles to U.S. Highway 90 in Gretna.

23. Cross U.S. Highway 90 and continue on C.R. 268 for 2.2 more miles to C.R. 379A.

24. Turn left on C.R. 379A and go 3 miles to C.R. 483.

25. Turn right on C.R. 483 and go 2.9 miles to C.R 267.

26. Turn right on C.R. 267 and go four-tenths of a mile to C.R. 272.

27. Turn left on C.R. 272 and go 1.7 miles to S.R. 65.

28. Turn right on S.R. 65 and go 3.8 miles to U.S. Highway 90 in Quincy.

29. Turn right on U.S. Highway 90 and go four-tenths of a mile to parking lot and end of route.

▲ Suwannee County loop

Here's a ride that begins and ends on the banks of the Suwannee River and spends all but a few yards in Suwannee County. This 108-mile loop is designed for a two-day trip.

The starting point is White Springs, a picturesque town in Hamilton County. Its population is well under 1,000, but it has a long history. Two interstate highways are only a few miles away, but White Springs is so quiet visitors feel as if they've left civilization behind them.

Park your car in front of Adams Country Store, an abandoned building a short distance from the Suwannee River. Made famous by Stephen Foster's song, this scenic stream flows south from Georgia, through North Florida and into the Gulf of Mexico. It has long been a favorite of canoeists.

Suwannee County is across the river from White Springs. You'll spend the next two days there. The county is bordered on the west and north by the Suwannee River.

The county seat of Suwannee County is Live Oak, which you'll visit on your return trip to White Springs. Poultry is the chief source of income in Suwannee, and 650,000 chickens are processed there every week. Pecans, watermelons and tobacco are the major crops; timber also is important.

Four miles out of White Springs you'll turn onto County Road 137 — one of the quietest stretches of road in Florida. It runs for more than 27 miles through wooded country interspersed with only a few houses. The road is in good condition, and after several miles without any traffic, bikers get the feeling they're riding on their own private highway.

About a mile before leaving C.R. 137 there's a road

The Suwannee River

turning left into Ichetucknee Springs State Park. It's a favorite spot for tubing, but you might want to plan a visit there for another day. The first day's ride is 75 miles; there's not much time for tubing.

There's a three-mile stretch on U.S. Highway 27 after leaving C.R. 137, but it's not busy. From there to the end of the first day's ride, the roads are quiet.

Be sure to carry enough water with you on this trip. There are only two towns along the first day's route. The first, Wellborn, is six miles south of C.R. 137. The second, O'Brien, is at the junction of U.S. Highway 129 and C.R. 349. There are stores in both locations.

The only rough stretch of road on the entire loop is the four miles on Howell Road before reaching O'Brien. You might have trouble finding the road. It's unmarked. Remember to turn left on the second hard-surfaced road on your left after leaving U.S. Highway 27. It's Howell Road, and it becomes C.R. 349 when it reaches O'Brien.

Dowling Park is an ideal spot to end the first day's ride. It's in an isolated location on the Suwannee River, but it's a scenic place to spend the night.

Operated by the Advent Christian Church, the

facilities have been here since the early 1970s. There's an attractive lodge that offers rooms for $30 per night for a single occupant, $35 for two. Nearby are dormitory accommodations for $7 per night and tent sites for $2 each. The latter, though, do not have showers. Meals are provided at a good cafeteria at reasonable prices.

Advance reservations are recommended here, since school, business and church groups frequently are spending weekends at Dowling Park.

The second day's return to White Springs will be an easy ride of about 33 miles.

From Dowling Park you'll be on C.R. 136 most of the way back to the starting point. Except for the traffic in Live Oak, you'll enjoy quiet roads again. There are a couple of turns in Live Oak to get you back onto C.R. 136, then it's smooth sailing all the way back to White Springs.

You'll be riding on the same 4.2 miles at the finish that you took when you began the ride.

There should be no problem in leaving your car in front of the country store. If you plan to spend the night in a motel before starting the ride, there is one in White Springs and a few more three miles away next to Interstate 75. You may choose to leave your car there.

The Stephen Foster State Folk Culture Center is just outside White Springs and is worth a visit.

After your short ride on the second day of the loop, you might want to look around White Springs. It's a pretty town with many old buildings and shaded streets. Bring your camera with you — there are plenty of photo opportunities here and more along C.R. 137 and at Dowling Park.

You're never far from the Suwannee River on this ride. After the first day's ride, you might want to rent a canoe for the day for $10 to explore the Suwannee.

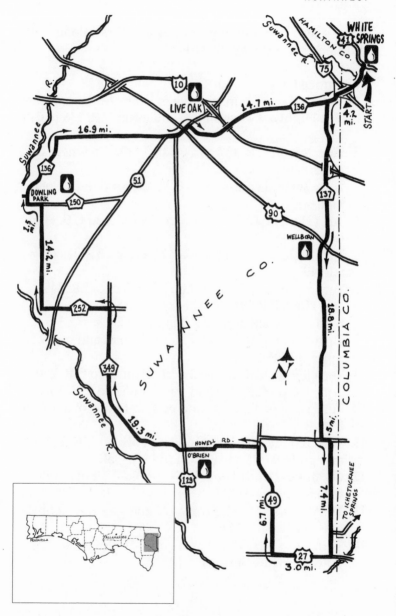

There's also a swimming pool at the park, along with shuffleboard and tennis courts.

Suwannee County loop
 1. From Adams Country Store in White Springs, cross U.S. Highway 41 and go 4.2 miles on C.R. 136 to C.R. 137.
 2. Turn left on C.R. 137 and go 18.8 miles to where C.R. 137 ends.
 3. Turn left and continue on C.R. 137 for one-half of a mile.
 4. Turn right on C.R. 137 and go 7.4 miles to U.S. Highway 27.
 5. Turn right on U.S. Highway 27 and go 3 miles to S.R. 49.
 6. Turn right on S.R. 49 and go 6.7 miles to C.R. 349 and Howell Road. It's the second hard-surfaced road on the left after U.S. Highway 27.
 7. Turn left on C.R. 349 and Howell Road and go 19.3 miles to C.R. 252.
 8. Turn left on C.R. 252 and go 14.2 miles to C.R. 250.
 9. Turn left on C.R. 250 and go 1.5 miles to C.R. 136.
10. Turn right on C.R. 136 and go two-tenths of a mile to Dowling Park.
11. Turn left after leaving Dowling Park on C.R. 136 and go 16.9 miles to S.R. 51 in Live Oak.
12. Go straight ahead on S.R. 51 for one-half of a mile to U.S. Highway 129.
13. Turn left on U.S. Highway 129 and go seven-tenths of a mile to C.R. 136.
14. Turn right on C.R. 136 and go 14.7 miles to starting point in White Springs.

▲ Tallahassee -St. Marks-Wakulla Springs loop

The state's first completed Rails to Trails bike route, a lighthouse built more than 170 years ago and one of the world's largest and deepest freshwater springs are included in an intriguing loop that begins and ends at the south end of Tallahassee.

Officially opened late in 1988, the 16-mile trail is a biker's dream. It's about 8 feet wide and heads straight as an arrow through the piney woods until stopping at the picturesque fishing village of St. Marks. A covered terminal with parking spaces for about 30 cars is at the starting point near Tallahassee.

This trail was built over the old roadbed of the Seaboard Coastline Railroad, which abandoned its spur line to St. Marks several years ago. After a long legal battle with landowners next to the railroad bed, the biking enthusiasts finally prevailed. The U.S. Department of Natural Resources joined forces with the Florida Department of Transportation to build this terrific trail. Bikers and joggers from the Tallahassee area can be found using this facility almost any time of the day.

The trail runs parallel to County Road 363 all the way and is just a few feet from the road. It ends in St. Marks, a town with about 350 people. There are several marinas and seafood restaurants in town. It is on the St. Marks River, which flows into the Gulf of Mexico four miles south of town.

At the trail's end, which is restricted only to cyclists and joggers, you have several options.

If you only want to ride the trail and briefly explore St. Marks, the ride is 32 miles. If you want to explore further, a ride to St. Marks Lighthouse is recommended. It's about 16 miles to the lighthouse from St. Marks and

Wakulla Springs Lodge

naturally enough, 16 miles back to town. That would add 32 miles to the ride, making this trip a 64-mile day.

It would be a shame not to include Wakulla Springs on this ride. You can take a side trip there, then return to the trail and end up with about 72 miles. Or you can skip the lighthouse trip, ride the trail to St. Marks, then make the swing over to Wakulla Springs and return on the trail to have a 46-mile day.

The entire route is within Leon and Wakulla counties. Leon County — with the state capital and Florida State University — has become a large metropolitan area. But Wakulla is one of Florida's least populated counties. More than half the county is covered by the Apalachicola National Forest, so its population is only about 10,000. The county seat is in Crawfordville, and that town is one of just two county seats in Florida that never incorporated.

If you opt for the side trips to both the lighthouse and the springs, be sure to bring your camera. It's a beautiful trip.

Less than three miles after leaving U.S. Highway 98 on C.R. 59, you'll enter the St. Marks National Wildlife Refuge. Shortly after that you'll come to the Visitor Center; make sure you stop there.

The center presents an overview of what there is to do and see at the refuge. There are trails for hiking, wildlife observation and photography. The people at the center are helpful and will provide information on wildlife sightings.

Hours for the center are 8 a.m. to 4:15 p.m. Monday through Friday and 10 a.m. to 5 p.m. on Saturday and Sunday. There are several informative displays in the center that describe refuge wildlife and habitats.

It's about seven miles from the center to the light-house. Many cyclists like to get an early start to see the wildlife. Get a map at the center to find out where the hiking trails and dikes are located. Wildlife is especially plentiful in the fall and winter.

The lighthouse, built in 1829, now is a national historic site. It was built then by Winslow Lewis of Boston for $11,765. The building wasn't accepted because the tower walls were hollow. It was rebuilt in 1831 and then again with a brand-new tower in 1842, when the soil began to erode under the tower.

The limestone block tower sits on a base 12 feet deep. It is 80 feet tall, and its walls are 4 feet thick at the base and taper to 18 inches at the top. The light, now electri-cally powered, can be seen 15 miles away. Its reflector lens, built in Paris and installed in 1829, resembles a large glass pineapple.

During the Civil War, Federal troops blockaded the

Apalachee Bay beyond the lighthouse and stray shells hit the tower and dwelling, burning the woodwork. Early in March of 1865 a Federal fleet of 16 ships anchored just off the lighthouse. On March 4 the lighthouse was mined by retreating Confederates, and the next day from 600 to 1,000 Federal soldiers landed at the lighthouse and began a march to capture Tallahassee. The plan was thwarted by the citizens of Woodville, about 10 miles north of St. Marks, in the Battle of Natural Bridge. A year after the war the house and tower were rebuilt.

In 1960 the light became automatic, triggered by an electric eye. The U.S. Coast Guard maintains the light, and the staff from the wildlife refuge maintain the house and grounds.

Much of the land surrounding the lighthouse is salt marshes. After you leave U.S. Highway 98 and turn onto C.R. 59, you'll ride about three miles through wooded areas, then pedal seven miles through marsh land to the lighthouse. Some spectacular photos have been taken along this road all the way to the lighthouse and throughout the wildlife refuge.

It's not necessary to return all the way to St. Marks after visiting the National Wildlife Refuge and the lighthouse. You can return to the bike trail in less than three miles after returning to U.S. Highway 98. Ride about three miles on the trail to C.R. 267 and exit there on the highway. From here to the Edward Ball Wakulla Springs State Park there's a wide shoulder lane for bikes for the entire 4.9 miles.

This park, originally owned by Edward Ball, a prominent official in the DuPont empire and a dominant figure in Florida politics for many years, was left to the state by Ball and turned into a state park of spectacular natural beauty.

St. Marks Lighthouse

A lavish 27-room Spanish-style lodge was built in 1937 by Ball. It features marble floors, ornate ceilings and antique furniture.

Ball used the area around the springs as a private hunting and fishing retreat for himself and guests.

After Ball's death, the lodge and dining facility became a conference center that is operated by the Florida State University for Professional Development and Public Service. A dining room, soda fountain, gift shop and guest rooms are open to the public. All guest rooms have private marble bathrooms.

Near the lodge is the entrance to the springs. The spring is the highlight of the 2,860-acre park. On April 11, 1973, a record peak flow from the spring was measured to be an amazing 14,325 gallons per second.

Explorers mapped the cavern in 1958 but only 1,100 feet into the cave's mouth. At that point, 250 feet underwater, the divers said their lights showed an ever-deepening, ever-widening cavern.

There are glass-bottom boats that take visitors on 30-minute tours downstream among ancient cypress trees and a remarkable abundance of wildlife. From these boats visitors can clearly see to the entrance of the cavern 120 feet below.

Wildlife is a major attraction in this natural setting. There are nine species of herons and egrets, along with hundreds of roosting black and turkey vultures, anhingas, swallow-tailed kites, osprey, bald eagles, limpkins and gallinules. In the winter there are between 1,000 and 2,000 waterfowl, mostly American widgeon, lesser scaup and American coot.

If you've pedaled all the way to St. Marks, then to the lighthouse and now to Wakulla Springs, you should be ready for a swim. There are bathhouse facilities available,

Wakulla Springs

but you are cautioned to swim only in a designated swimming area at the head spring. Venture outside this area and it could be quite dangerous. The Wakulla River is home to a great variety of wildlife, including alligators. Stay in the designated swimming area so you'll be sure to have both feet for the ride back to Tallahassee.

The park is open from 8 a.m. to sunset every day. It's about five miles from the park back to the bike trail, and then another 10 miles to the end of the trail.

This is a delightful trip and an exposure to a Florida that is still much the same as when the Timucuan Indians were the only residents. Don't miss it!

Tallahassee-St. Marks-Wakulla Springs loop

1. Travel on the Tallahassee/St. Marks Rail-Trail for 16 miles.
2. Turn left at end of bicycle trail and go one block on

Riverside Drive to C.R. 363.

3. Turn left on C.R. 363 and go 2.6 miles to U.S. Highway 98.
4. Turn right on U.S. Highway 98 and go 2.5 miles to C.R. 59.
5. Turn right on C.R. 59 and go 10.5 miles to St. Marks Lighthouse.
6. Turn around at lighthouse and return on C.R. 59 to U.S. Highway 98.
7. Turn left on U.S. Highway 98 and go 2.8 miles to bike trail.
8. Turn right on bike trail and go 3 miles to C.R. 267.
9. Turn left on C.R. 267 and go 4.9 miles to Edward Ball Wakulla Springs State Park.
10. Continue on park road 1.7 miles to Wakulla Springs.
11. Return to entrance to park and turn right on C.R. 267.
12. Go 4.9 miles back to bicycle trail and turn left.
13. Go remaining 10.5 miles on bicycle trail to terminal in Tallahassee and end of route.

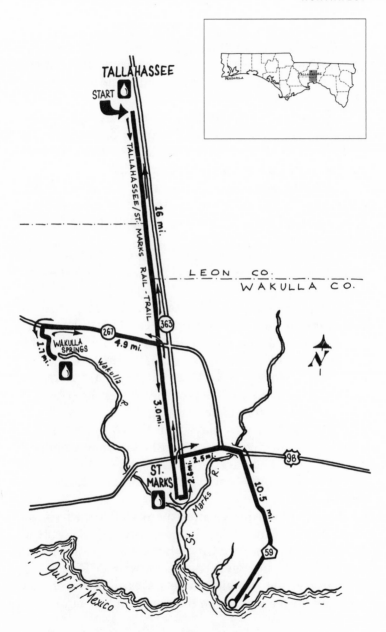

TALLAHASSEE

START

TALLAHASSEE/ST. MARKS RAIL-TRAIL

16 mi.

LEON CO.
WAKULLA CO.

267

4.9 mi.

363

WAKULLA
SPRINGS

1.7 mi.

Wakulla R.

3.0 mi.

N

98

2.5 mi.

ST.
MARKS

2.6 mi.

10.5 mi.

St. Marks R.

59

St. Marks R.

Gulf of Mexico

NORTHWEST
PENSACOLA
TALLAHASSEE

65

▲ White Springs-Jasper loop

Hamilton County is another sparsely settled county in North Florida, but it's scenic country and a wonderful place for biking.

The historic Suwannee River forms the county's eastern and southern borders, and another pretty river, the Withlacoochee, is its western border. The Florida-Georgia line marks the county's northern edge.

With so much of the county on the Suwannee River, it's natural that it is the home of the Stephen Foster State Folk Culture Center. This state-owned center will be on your route.

Because the route is only 56 miles, it will give you time to visit the center and enjoy this ride through beautiful, isolated countryside.

Park your car in front of Adams Country Store in White Springs; it's a short distance on U.S. Highway 41.

Less than a mile from the start you'll arrive at the Stephen Foster Center. There's a small admission fee, but the center definitely is worth a visit. There are dioramas and other exhibits that depict the scenes described in some of Foster's more famous songs.

A piano that was played by the composer is displayed, along with the desk where he sat while arranging his song, " Old Folks at Home." The song is better known as " Suwannee River " and has been Florida's official state song since 1935.

Foster, despite his legacy of many well-known songs, was a tragic figure. He died alone, with only 38 cents in his pocket in New York City when he was 37. He never visited Florida and never saw the Suwannee River.

Besides the exhibits, there's a carillon tower that rings out Foster's music on the hour and half-hour.

Boat tours on the Suwannee and guided tours of the tower and visitor center are available daily, though the boat tours are available only when the water level is acceptably high.

There's an old-fashioned Fourth of July celebration at the center each year, and the Florida Folk Festival is held there annually.

Established in 1827, Hamilton County is one of Florida's oldest. It was named for Alexander Hamilton. Phosphate mining is big here, and 80 percent of the county is commercial timberland.

There are less than 10,000 people living in Hamilton County, so you'll see few houses on the loop from White Springs to Jasper.

Jasper, with a population of slightly more than 2,000, is the county seat.

The roads to Jasper are lightly traveled, and there is minimal traffic during the last 30 miles of your ride. It's possible to travel the stretch of 14 miles on County Road 135 without seeing a single vehicle. It's a pleasure to ride through this heavily wooded country, and it's equally as pleasurable to travel the 14-mile stretch on State Road 6 before that.

You might want to jump in the Suwannee River when you finish your ride. There are several good swimming holes up and down its banks. Canoes also may be rented here.

There are two other routes starting from White Springs, but they are much longer and will take most cyclists at least two days. This one easily can be handled in a single day.

Be sure you carry enough water. The only place you'll be able to fill your water bottles after leaving White Springs will be in Jasper. That's more than 25 miles away and it could be rough on one of those sweltering, summer days.

White Springs-Jasper loop

1. Turn right on U.S. Highway 41 from front of Adams Country Store and go two-tenths of a mile to C.R. 25A, first road past Majik Market.
2. Turn left on C.R. 25A and go 11.4 miles to C.R. 132.
3. Turn left on C.R. 132 and go 1.5 miles to U.S. Highway 129.
4. Turn right on U.S. Highway 129 and go 2.2 miles to C.R. 158.
5. Turn left on C.R. 158 and go 5.8 miles to C.R. 249.
6. Turn right on C.R. 249 and go 5.5 miles to where C.R. 249 intersects U.S. Highway 129 and S.R. 6 in Jasper.
7. Continue on S.R. 6 for 14.1 miles to C.R. 135.
8. Turn right on C.R. 135 and go 15.1 miles to U.S. Highway 41.
9. Turn right on U.S. Highway 41 and go one-half of a mile to junction with C.R. 136 and starting point.

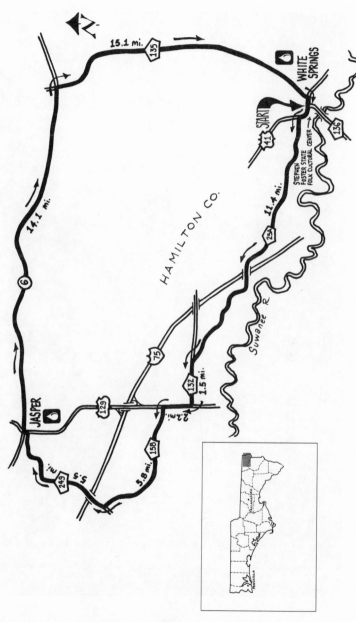

Stephen Foster State Folk Culture Center

▲ White Springs-Jasper-Live Oak loop

A ride of more than 100 miles through the back roads of Hamilton, Madison and Suwannee counties will acquaint you with the scenery and solitude of North Florida.

This route measures 113.4 miles, starts and finishes in White Springs or Jasper and gives you an opportunity to cross and take a close look at both the Withlacoochee and Suwannee rivers.

You have an option of starting at either White Springs or Jasper, both in Hamilton County. If you start at White Springs, the ride from there to Dowling Park in Suwannee County will be 81.4 miles on the first day; leaving 32 miles to complete the loop on the second day. If you start your ride in Jasper, it's 51.4 miles to Dowling Park, which would leave 62 miles for the second day's ride.

Dowling Park is recommended as an overnight stop if you don't plan to complete the route in a single day.

Whether you start in White Springs or Jasper, you'll spend almost the entire time in wide-open country. It's scenic, but it's isolated. The route travels through wooded areas and farmland. There are few houses along the route and even fewer stores.

Be sure you're well-supplied with water and snacks when you leave. The only towns along the route, other than White Springs and Jasper, are Live Oak, the county seat of Suwannee County, and Lee, a town with a population of about 300 in Madison County.

For cyclists who want to break the trip into a two-day ride and don't want to stay at Dowling Park, you can camp at the Suwannee River State Park. It's about nine miles east of Lee at the junction of the Withlacoochee and Suwannee rivers. Though there are restroom facilities, there are no showers.

The park opens at 8 a.m. and closes at sunset each day. There is a fee for camping. There's an overlook for getting a panoramic view of the two rivers and surrounding wooded uplands. Springs may be seen bubbling from the banks when the water level is low.

An earthworks built by the Confederates to protect the railroad bridges across the Suwannee River can be seen south of the junction of the rivers. Supplies needed to feed the Confederate armies were shipped by rail into Georgia. Union troops, sent from Jacksonville to capture the bridge, were repulsed near Olustee in the only battle of the war fought on Florida soil.

The Suwannee River State Park is on your left shortly after you pass the State Agricultural Inspection Station on U.S. Highway 90.

The route soon turns south onto River Road in Suwannee County. Because the road is unmarked, note that it is the first road on your right after crossing the Suwannee River. Florida Power Company has a sign there about the Suwannee Power Plant.

It's an 11-mile ride from there to Dowling Park.

If you begin your ride in White Springs, leave your car in front of Adams Country Store. If your starting point is Jasper, leave your car behind the police station, a short distance from the starting point at the junction of County Road 6 and U.S. Highway 129.

Those traveling to North Florida from other parts of the state might want to stay in a motel the night before starting the ride. There are good motels and restaurants in both towns.

If you're starting from White Springs and spend the night in Dowling Park, your second day will end early enough to give you enough time to visit the Stephen

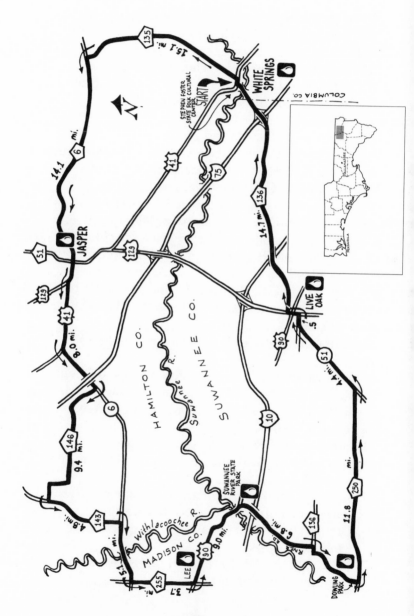

Foster State Folk Culture Center, about a mile outside of White Springs. It's operated by the state.

White Springs-Jasper-Live Oak loop

1. Turn left on U.S. Highway 41 from front of Adams Country Store in White Springs and go one-half of a mile to C.R. 135.
2. Turn left on C.R. 135 and go 15.1 miles to C.R. 6.
3. Turn left on C.R. 6 and go 14.1 miles to intersection with U.S. Highway 129 in Jasper.
4. Continue on C.R. 6 for 8 miles to C.R. 146.
5. Turn right on C.R. 146 and go 9.4 miles to C.R. 143.
6. Turn left on C.R. 143 and go 4.8 miles to S.R. 6.
7. Turn right on S.R. 6 and go 5.1 miles to C.R. 255.
8. Turn left on C.R. 255 and go 3.7 miles to U.S. Highway 90 in Lee.
9. Turn left on U.S. Highway 90 and go 9 miles to River Road, just past the State Agricultural Inspection Station.
10. Turn right on River Road and go 6.8 miles to C.R. 136.
11. Turn right on C.R. 136 and go 4.6 miles to Dowling Park (a suggested stopping point for the first day).
12. Turn right out of Dowling Park and go three-tenths of a mile to C.R. 250.
13. Turn left on C.R. 250 and go 11.8 miles to S.R. 51.
14. Turn left on S.R. 51 and go 4.4 miles to traffic light in Live Oak.
15. Turn right at traffic light and continue on S.R. 51 for one-half of a mile to U.S. Highway 129.
16. Turn left on U.S Highway 129 and go six-tenths of a mile to C.R. 136.
17. Turn right on C.R. 136 and go 14.7 miles to starting point in White Springs.

▲ Perry-Steinhatchee -Mayo loop

Enjoy this loop that features deserted roads, lovely views of the Gulf of Mexico, thick woods and a visit to a picturesque fishing village. The ride begins and ends in Perry and covers 110.6 miles.

Perry is 50 miles southeast of Tallahassee and 135 miles west of Jacksonville. It's the county seat of Taylor County, which bills itself as the Tree Capital. There are 673,300 acres in Taylor County, and 90 per cent of those acres are covered by forests.

This loop will take you past miles and miles of trees, mostly pine. And the forests don't stop in Taylor County; they continue into Lafayette County for more than 50 miles.

There are no hills or traffic on this loop, so some cyclists might want to complete the ride in a single day. But for those who like to explore and enjoy a good seafood dinner, an overnight stop in Steinhatchee is recommended.

Steinhatchee is tucked away at the extreme southern end of Taylor County on the Steinhatchee River, just a short walk from the Gulf of Mexico. There are outstanding seafood restaurants in town and several motels and campgrounds. It's 40 miles from Perry. A stop for the night here will leave 70 miles for the second day's ride.

Those 40 miles from Perry to Steinhatchee are interesting even though you're in isolated country most of the time. Just before leaving Perry you'll pass the Forest Capital State Museum on U.S. Highway 19-98. It's open daily from 9 a.m. to 5:30 p.m.

Though U.S. Highway 19-98 is a busy route, there's an extra lane on the right. Stay in that and you won't be bothered by the traffic. Even after that extra lane ends 1.3

miles before you turn onto County Road 361, it's a divided four-lane highway. There may be some confusion in locating C.R. 361. It's not marked, but it's the first paved road to the right after you see a green sign pointing to Keaton Beach.

From here to Steinhatchee, you'll be on a road that is almost devoid of traffic. It's forest on both sides of the road for 17 miles until you reach Keaton Beach. The road takes a sharp turn to the left here, but a short ride on a side road to Keaton Beach is worthwhile. The town is on the Gulf with several seafood restaurants, marinas and motels. It's not as large as Steinhatchee, but it's quaint and you can park your bike and walk around. People are friendly, and they can supply interesting information about the area.

It's another 19 miles to Steinhatchee. A Spaniard, Panfila de Navaez, is believed to have come through here with 300 men in 1529, and Hernando De Soto visited the area in 1539. They found neither gold nor silver, but they did convert the Timucuan Indians to Christianity.

After leaving Steinhatchee you'll be on S.R. 51 for more than 30 miles. This road cuts across a small portion of Dixie County, but it's all Lafayette County after that.

You'll leave the wilderness behind you as the route enters Mayo. This is the county seat of Lafayette County, a county with less than 5,000 people. Corn, cotton, peanuts and tobacco are grown here, and the manufacturing of lumber and wood products also is important.

The roads in this county also are quiet. You will leave S.R. 51 a few miles north of Mayo when you turn onto C.R. 543B. It's a good road, but there are two miles of rough slag construction before it crosses U.S. Highway 27.

Your last 15 miles will be on U.S. Highway 27. It used to be a very busy road, but when Interstate 10 was built a few miles north, it drew most of the through traffic. There will be more traffic than you have experienced on the other roads of the loop, but it's not dangerous. Riders should wear bright clothing just to be safe. After 12.5 miles, the road becomes four-lane on the outskirts of Perry.

If you're not comfortable with 12.5 miles on two-lane U.S. Highway 27, you might want to switch to U.S. Highway 19-98. It's a four-lane divided highway, and you'll intersect it on S.R. 51 a few miles north of Steinhatchee. It's a straight shot to Perry from there and will give you a 35-mile second day. The traffic on U.S. Highway 19-98 is heavier, but the vehicles have that extra lane to get past you.

The police in Perry will let you leave your car behind the police station.

Hotel and restaurant accommodations in Perry are plentiful. This was a major stopping point for Florida visitors before the interstate highways were built. Some tourists still pass through here, and the county attracts many Florida residents interested in hunting and fishing in Taylor County.

Perry has a population of 10,000, which accounts for just about half of the county's total. Proctor and Gamble operates a big cellulose plant that employs 1,100 people. The biggest event staged here each year is the Florida Forest Festival. It lasts four weeks in October and attracts an average 50,000 visitors. Another highlight is the World's Largest Free Fish Fry. Three and a half tons of fried mullet, a half-ton of hushpuppies and 240 gallons of baked beans are served to 10,000 luncheon guests each year.

Perry-Steinhatchee-Mayo loop

1. Turn left on Jefferson Street after leaving Perry police

station and go 1.2 miles to U.S. Highway 19-98.
2. Turn left on U.S. Highway 19-98 and go 3.9 miles to C.R. 361.
3. Turn right on C.R. 361 and go 17.3 miles to where C.R. 361 turns left toward Steinhatchee.
4. Continue on C.R. 361 for 18.9 miles to Steinhatchee.
5. Turn left in Steinhatchee on S.R. 51 and go 35.4 miles to C.R. 534B. This is 2.3 miles past U.S. Highway 27 in Mayo.
6. Turn left on C.R. 534B and go 7.4 miles to where C.R. 534B turns right. Continue on C.R. 534B for 5.4 miles to C.R. 348.
7. Turn left on C.R. 348 and go 4.4 miles to U.S. Highway 27. C.R. 348 is unmarked, but it is first road on left after crossing U.S. Highway 27.
8. Turn right on U.S. Highway 27 and go 16.3 miles to U.S. Highway 221 (Jefferson Street) in Perry.
9. Turn right on Jefferson Street and go 1.2 miles to starting point at police station.

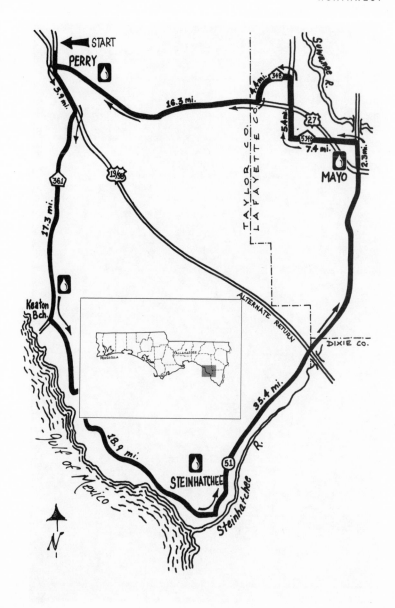

START

PERRY

5.9 mi.

16.3 mi.

.44 mi. 348

Suwannee R.

.54 mi. 27

.53 mi.

7.4 mi.

2.3 mi.

MAYO

19/98

361

17.3 mi.

TAYLOR CO.

LAFAYETTE CO.

ALTERNATE RETURN

DIXIE CO.

Keaton Bch.

PENSACOLA

TALLAHASSEE

35.4 mi.

18.9 mi.

51

Steinhatchee R.

STEINHATCHEE

Gulf of Mexico

N

Ginny Springs

2. North

▲ Devil's Millhopper loop (near Gainesville)

Two miles northwest of Gainesville is the only geological site in the state park system. The Devil's Millhopper is a good starting point for a day's ride through the rural roads of Alachua, Gilchrist, Columbia and Union counties.

If your starting point is the Devil's Millhopper, it's a ride of about 75 miles. The park opens at 9 a.m., so early starters might want to park their cars elsewhere. A good parking spot nearby is the Northwood Banking Center, on U.S. Highway 441, about two miles from the Devil's Millhopper on County Road 232.

The Devil's Millhopper is a large sinkhole that formed when a cavern roof collapsed. The sinkhole measures 500 feet from rim to rim and tapers to 100 feet at the bottom — 120 feet down. Visitors have been coming here since the 1880s to marvel at the sight of streams running down the steep slopes of the sinkhole, only to disappear through crevices in the floor. Researchers have found fossil shark teeth and marine shells, which indicate a large sea covered the area eons ago. Upper layers of the sinkhole have revealed remains of extinct land animals.

There are exhibits explaining the natural history of the site, and guided walks are provided weekly. The site is in a heavily wooded area, and those starting the ride from here might want to spend some time exploring before or after their ride. If you start from the bank parking lot, it will be handy to stop at the site on your return. For further information write to Devil's Millhopper State Geological Site, 4732 N.W. 53rd Ave., Gainesville, Fla. 32601; (904) 336-2008.

From the bank parking lot to the Devil's Millhopper, the traffic on County Road 232 is fairly heavy, but there is a bike lane on the road and a bike path parallel to that for 1.5 miles. It's another half-mile to the geological site entrance, then a bicycle path resumes on the road for another half-mile. After that, there are about 2.5 miles with no bicycle lane or path. The traffic at this point usually is light, and large yellow signs indicate "Bicycles Sharing Highway." The bicycle lane resumes for the rest of the ride on C.R. 232.

After more than six miles, you'll arrive at San Felasco Hammock State Preserve on the left side of the road. This 6,500-acre site, bought in 1974 by the state, is a worthwhile stop. There's a nature trail south of C.R. 232, and ranger-led hikes are provided seasonally. Ask the park manager at Devil's Millhopper for a schedule and reservations.

At the 16-mile point on the route, you'll cross U.S. highways 27 and 41. Be careful—it's a busy intersection.

Devil's Millhopper

County Road 232 continues into Gilchrist County, one of Florida's most sparsely populated counties.

As you ride along C.R. 340 in Gilchrist, you'll see a side road to Ginnie Springs. It's a beautiful, natural setting and a great place for swimming, scuba diving and canoeing on the Santa Fe River. There's a large camping area with excellent facilities.

You will have covered about 33 miles of the route when you turn onto State Road 47. There's a gas station and store to the right that offers sandwiches, drinks and snacks. Take note, though, it's closed on Sunday.

It's another eight miles from there to Fort White, a town of about 350 in Columbia County. Before entering Fort White, you'll cross the Santa Fe River. There's a small picnic area next to the river.

Turn right onto U.S. Highway 27 at the convenience store in Fort White and travel for a short distance before heading into more rural country on C.R. 18.

The route cuts through a corner of Union County before heading south into Alachua County and the town of Alachua. This is a town of about 4,000 and offers a variety of places to stop for a meal or a snack. Be careful crossing four-lane U.S. Highway 441. There's a block of renovated businesses after you cross that's good for browsing and strolling.

Just after entering the town of Alachua, C.R. 235 joins C.R. 241 and may cause some confusion. Continue straight ahead. The roads join through town then branch off south of Alachua. Turn left onto C.R. 241 and take that road all the way back to C.R. 232. You'll find some hills here.

When you return to C.R. 232, you'll be retracing the route you followed for the first eight miles of the ride. You'll have a bicycle lane for 3.5 miles, then no lane for a little more than two miles. The final stretch back to the bank or the geological site will have a bike lane.

This route starts almost within sight of the University of Florida, then meanders through some of the most sparsely populated areas of the state. There's very little traffic, and the road conditions are good. Some of the best scenery is at the start and finish on C.R. 232, where large trees form a canopy over the road.

While the route can be traveled by most bikers in one day, those who want to spend some time at the Devil's Millhopper and San Felasco will prefer to break it into a two-day outing. Those making a full weekend of the route can camp at Ginnie Springs campgrounds near Ichetucknee Springs State Park or O'leno State Park in Fort White.

Devil's Millhopper loop

1. Turn left out of Northwood Banking Center on C.R. 232 and go 8.5 miles to C. R. 241. If starting from the

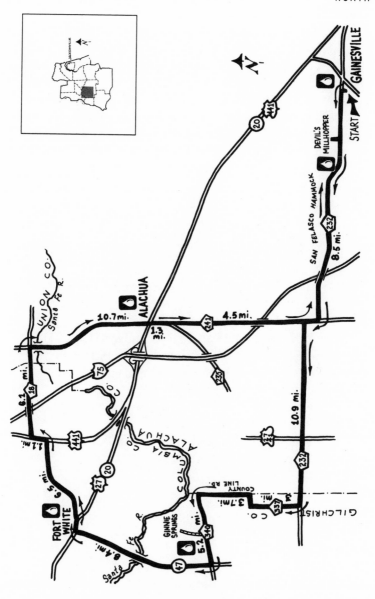

Devil's Millhopper, turn right and go 6.5 miles to C.R 241.

2. Turn right on C.R. 241 and go eight-tenths of a mile to C.R. 232.
3. Turn left on C.R. 232 and go 10.9 miles to C.R. 337. It's the first paved road after entering Gilchrist County.
4. Turn right on C.R. 337 and go 3 miles to right turn in the road. It's still C.R. 337 for another mile.
5. Turn left on C.R. 2085 (County Line Road) and go 3.7 miles to C.R. 340.
6. Turn left on C.R. 340 and go 5.2 miles to S.R. 47.
7. Turn right on S.R. 47 and go 8.4 miles to U.S. Highway 27 in the town of Fort White.
8. Turn right on U.S. Highway 27 and go two-tenths of a mile to C.R. 18.
9. Turn left on C.R. 18 and go 6.5 miles to U.S. Highway 441.
10. Turn left on U.S. Highway 441 and go 1.1 miles to C.R. 18.
11. Turn right on C.R. 18 and go 6.1 miles to C.R. 241.
12. Turn right on C.R. 241 and go 10.7 miles to where C.R. 235 intersects in the town of Alachua.
13. Continue on C.R. 241 and 235 for 1.3 miles to where road splits. Take C.R. 241 to the left and continue for 4.5 miles to C.R. 232.
14. Turn left on C.R. 232 and go 8.5 miles back to the starting point in the bank parking lot.

▲*Ichetucknee Springs loop*

While Ichetucknee Springs State Park is best known for tubing, it also is a good starting and stopping point for a back roads biking tour of North Florida.

The bike tour is about 66 miles. You can leave your car at the park and complete the tour in a day. The park, which charges a small entrance fee, is open daily from 8 a.m. to sunset.

Established as a state park in a heavily wooded area of Columbia County northwest of Gainesville in 1970, Ichetucknee entices hundreds of people eager to unwind — and cool off — on a leisurely six-mile float downriver. Water temperature is 73 degrees.

A series of springs form the Ichetucknee River, which flows southwest before joining the Sante Fe River. The average total flow of the springs is about 233 million gallons of water daily.

The springs have a long and colorful history. Indians hunted and fished here; a Spanish mission once was located on the riverbank, and travelers on the historic Bellamy Road quenched their thirst with its cool water. In the early part of this century, phosphate was extracted from small surface mines.

Before your bike ride you may want to explore a nature trail that winds through a hardwood hammock along the river. After the ride, though, you probably will be investing in one of those tubes. It's a great reward for a hard day of pedaling.

This tour winds through areas with quiet roads and very little population. The roads are in good condition. Your only problem may be the lack of signs at some turns.

Watch carefully for the only sign — a little hand-painted marker attached to a fence — alerting you to your

Tubing at Ichetucknee Springs

right turn off State Road 47 onto County Road 240. It's in a little hamlet called Columbia City. You'll encounter another problem with S.R. 238 before entering the town of Providence. You'll need to turn left there from C.R. 245, but the road is not marked. There is, however, a sign at the corner for the Old Providence Baptist Church. It will be on your left. Turn left there, and you'll be on your way.

Providence, in the southwest corner of Union County, has a country store and a few other businesses. It will be the 25-mile mark on your ride and a good spot to grab a cold drink.

Shortly after leaving Providence, you'll turn south into Alachua County on C.R. 241.

At the 44-mile mark you'll enter High Springs, a town with a population of about 2,500. U.S. highways 41 and 441 go through High Springs, and before the interstate highway system was built, this town was a major tourist stop. Several motels still are operating, but No Vacancy signs rarely are seen.

If you're stopping for lunch, there's an above-average restaurant, the Great Outdoors Inc., on your way.

At the southern edge of High Springs, the route turns west onto C.R. 340. You'll have a little more than eight miles before turning onto S.R. 47 where there's a store that offers cold drinks and snacks.

From this crossroads, little more than 14 miles remain to Ichetucknee. You'll ride through the small town of Fort White just before leaving S.R. 47 and returning to your starting point at the state park.

This route travels through four counties and offers a variety of wooded areas as well as agricultural land that produces corn, watermelons, hay, truck crops and tobacco. Union County, which you ride through briefly, is the smallest county in Florida and the site of the state prison at Raiford.

Ichetucknee Springs and the area surrounding it are largely unchanged from the days when Indians roamed

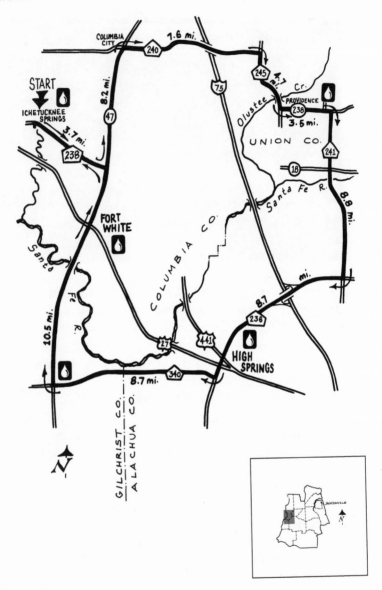

this part of Florida.

Though there are no camping facilities in the state park, private campgrounds along the road leading to the park offer good facilities for those who plan to spend a weekend in the area. Campgrounds also will allow you to park your car while you're touring the area by bicycle.

Ichetucknee Springs loop

1. Turn right on S.R. 238 out of Ichetucknee Springs State Park and go 3.7 miles to S.R. 47.
2. Turn left on S.R. 47 and go 8.2 miles to C.R. 240.
3. Turn right on C.R. 240 and go 7.6 miles to C.R. 245.
4. Turn right on C.R. 245 and go 4.7 miles to C.R. 238.
5. Turn left on C.R. 238 and go 3.5 miles to C.R. 241.
6. Turn right on C.R. 241 and go 8.8 miles to C.R. 236.
7. Turn right on C.R. 236 and go 8.7 miles through the town of High Springs to C.R. 340.
8. Turn right on C.R. 340 and go 8.7 miles to S.R. 47.
9. Turn right on S.R. 47 and go 10.5 miles to C.R. 238.
10. Turn left on C.R. 238 and go 3.7 miles back to the starting point at the entrance to the Ichetucknee Springs State Park.

▲Starke-Olustee-Lake City loop

A visit to the site of the only major Civil War battle in Florida is included in a two-day tour of the back roads of North Florida.

The 114-mile route travels through four counties and can be handled in a single day if you ride fast and don't stop long at the Olustee battlefield, now a state historic site.

Starke is the starting and stopping point for this sparsely settled loop. Much of it is over flat terrain and through wooded countryside, including the Osceola National Forest. There are long stretches where traffic is extremely light. At one point you will be within a short distance of the Florida State Prison.

If you're going to make it a two-day tour — and this is recommended — choose to stop either at the Ocean Pond Campground in the Osceola National Forest, about 42 miles from your starting point, or in Lake City, where there are plenty of motels to choose from. Lake City is 56.5 miles from Starke, which leaves 57.5 miles for the final day. The motels are bunched near U.S. Highway 441 and Interstate 75, an additional three or four miles off the route each way.

You'll encounter traffic in only two areas. The first is on State Road 121 between the towns of Raiford and Lake Butler. This is a stretch of 6.5 miles. It's not heavy traffic, and it's lighter on the weekends than during weekdays. The only other trouble spot is your last three miles into Starke on U.S. Highway 301. This is heavy traffic, moving at high speed, but it's a four-lane divided highway. The traffic is lighter on weekends, and you'd be riding it on Sunday if you decide on a two-day weekend trip.

There are frequent turns onto different roads, so pay close attention to the directions and the mileage figures. There are a few unmarked roads.

Start your ride at the Starke police station at the corner of Atkins and Clark streets. Turn left on Clark Street and go two blocks to Brownell Street (S.R. 16); you'll cross U.S. Highway 301 within one block. In a half-mile, you'll be in rural countryside, cycling down County Road 229 through wooded, scenic areas.

This road enters Raiford, a town of less than 300 people, but it's well-known throughout the state because of its proximity to the state prison. That sprawling institution is only a mile from town. All of the state's license plates are produced by inmates at the state prison.

Only a few miles before entering Raiford you'll leave Bradford County and enter Union County. Union County is the smallest in the state. It wasn't established until 1921, and more than 80 percent of the land is devoted to commercial forests.

After leaving Lake Butler, Union County's county seat and a town of about 2,000 population, you'll head into more isolated rural country on C.R. 231. You may not see any traffic on this road for 14.7 miles until you reach U.S. Highway 90 in the crossroads community of Olustee.

It's 2.6 miles from Olustee to the historic site of the battlefield. The park is open from 8 a.m. to 5 p.m. daily except Tuesday and Wednesday. An interesting museum in the interpretive center is open from 9 a.m. to 5 p.m. Thursday through Monday, and it's worth spending some time there.

The Battle of Olustee was fought on Feb. 20, 1864. A federal expedition was sent from Hilton Head, S.C., to occupy Jacksonville for a fourth time. The objectives were to cut communications between East and West Florida and deprive the Confederacy of food from East and South Florida. The federals also wanted to gain use of Florida cotton, turpentine and timber and gather recruits for Negro regiments.

The Federal force at Olustee was made up of 5,500 officers and men and 16 guns. Against this, the Confederate force was made up of 5,200 officers and men and 12 guns. Late in the day the Union troops withdrew, leaving behind 203 killed, 1,152 wounded and 506 missing. Confederate casualties were 93 killed, 847 wounded and six missing.

Complete details of the battle are provided in the museum and interpretive center.

From this historic site you'll retrace your route for a mile and a half before heading north toward the Osceola National Forest. Now you'll be in a heavily wooded area, mostly pine trees, with a good road and almost no traffic. The Ocean Pond Campground is on a large lake close to the site of the Battle of Olustee. There are 50 camp sites, hiking trails and restrooms and showers. Ocean Pond is a natural 1,760-acre lake and an excellent spot for swimming.

If you prefer a bed for the night, you'll have about 13 more miles to Lake City. In addition to all the motels there, you will have a wide choice of restaurants. To reach these motels and restaurants turn right on U.S. Highway 90 in downtown Lake City and ride about three miles.

When you start pedaling again the next morning return to the junction of U.S. Highway 441 and U.S. Highway 90. Turn right and go four-tenths of a mile to C.R. 10A. Now you're back on the route. The next turn — to C.R. 133 — is not marked. Watch for an S & S convenience store on your right. Turn right to enter C.R. 133. The road sign has it marked as Country Club Road.

You'll leave Columbia County on C.R. 241 and return to Union County. When C.R. 241 turns left onto C.R. 238, the town of Providence will be just about 200 yards on your right.

The remainder of the ride will be mostly on C.R. 18. It's a quiet little road that goes through the towns of Worthington Springs and Brooker. Both have only a few hundred residents but are typical of the crossroads communities that are scattered about most of the rural areas of North Florida. Many of the houses are old, but they're neat little villages that seem to enjoy being out of the mainstream of this fast-growing state. Not much happens here, and that's the way people seem to prefer it.

There will be a few miles on C.R. 227, and then three miles on U.S. Highway 301 before you return to your starting point.

Starke, with a population of about 6,000, is the county seat of Bradford County, named in honor of the first Florida officer to be killed in the Civil War. Timber, livestock and truck gardening are the major products in the county. Quite a few residents commute to jobs at the state prison.

This is a good two-day loop over lightly traveled roads, highlighted by the Olustee battlefield and the Osceola National Forest. It's strictly back roads Florida.

Starke-Olustee-Lake City loop

1. Turn left from Starke police station on Clark Street and go one-tenth of a mile (2 blocks) to Brownell Street.
2. Turn left on Brownell Street (S.R. 16), and go four-tenths of a mile to C.R. 229.
3. Turn left on C.R. 229 and go 11.4 miles to S.R. 121 in town of Raiford.
4. Turn left on S.R. 121 and go 6.5 miles to S.R. 100.
5. Turn right on S.R. 100, go through town of Lake Butler and 2.2 miles to C.R. 231.
6. Turn right on C.R. 231 and go 14.7 miles to U.S.

Highway 90 and the town of Olustee.

7. Turn right on U.S. Highway 90 and go 2.6 miles to Olustee battlefield.
8. Turn right from the battlefield on U.S. Highway 90 and go 1.4 miles to C.R. 250A. Road is unmarked, but it is the first road on right after leaving battlefield.
9. Turn right on C.R. 250A and go 7.4 miles to C.R. 250.
10. Turn left on C.R. 250 and go 10.7 miles to U.S. Highway 441.
11. Turn left at traffic light on U.S. Highway 441 and go 2.3 miles to C.R. 10A in Lake City.
12. Turn left on C.R. 10A and go 1.7 miles to C.R. 133.
13. Turn right on C.R. 133 and go 3.5 miles to C.R. 252.
14. Turn left on C.R. 252 and go 6.9 miles to C.R. 241.
15. Turn right on C.R. 241 and go 7.3 miles to C.R. 238.
16. Turn left on C.R. 238 and go 1.8 miles to C.R. 241.
17. Turn right on C.R. 241 and go 3.6 miles to C.R. 18. C.R. 241 is unmarked, but it is the road where sign and arrow point toward Alachua.
18. Turn left on C.R. 18 and go 5.1 miles to S.R. 121.
19. Turn right on S.R. 121 and go 1 mile to C.R. 18.
20. Turn left on C.R. 18 and go 6.6 miles to where C.R. 18 dead ends into C.R. 231 and C.R. 235.
21. Turn right at junction and go two-tenths of a mile to business street in town of Brooker.
22. Turn left on business street (which is C.R. 18), and go 9.7 miles to where C.R. 18 turns right.
23. Don't turn right but go straight ahead on C.R. 227.
24. Continue on C.R. 227 for 4 miles to U.S. Highway 301.
25. Turn left on U.S. Highway 301 and go 4 miles to end of route at corner of Atkins and Clark streets behind police station.

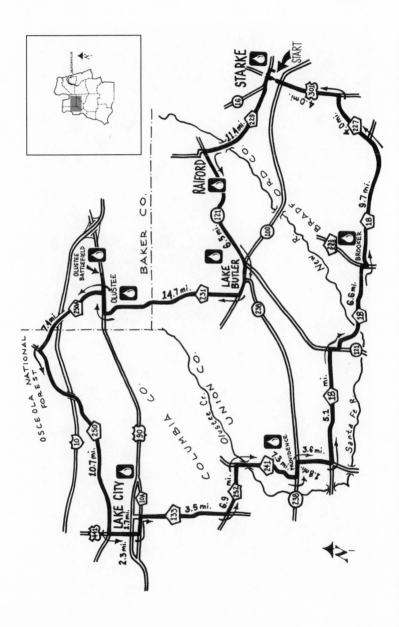

▲McIntosh-Morriston loop

McIntosh, one of the nicest towns in North Florida, is a good starting point for a 67-mile loop through Marion and Levy counties. You'll see some outstanding horse farms on your ride.

This pretty, oak-shaded village is only two miles from the Alachua County line, about halfway between Ocala and Gainesville. McIntosh was a rural Victorian community, and more than 30 homes date back to the 19th century. The town, with a population now of about 400, has done a good job of preserving its past and is converting an old railroad depot into a museum.

The starting point for this ride will be Van Ness Park, just two blocks east of busy U.S. Highway 441, a four-lane road that bisects the town. This shady park is the site of the McIntosh Civic Center. You may park your car here or at the post office a few blocks away if you are riding on a weekend.

Your route will head west out of McIntosh into gently rolling country, then turn south after a few miles.

While Marion County has been one of the fastest growing counties in the state in recent years, this part of the county has been largely unaffected by the population boom. The growth has been occurring in Ocala and areas south.

The area is sparsely populated, and the countryside is mostly wooded. Your first brush with civilization after leaving McIntosh will be the community of Flemington. It's not a town but a collection of houses and a country store that has been around longer than even the oldest residents. The store still is operating and offers snacks and cold drinks. It's closed on Sunday.

Refill your water bottles here — Flemington is the

last outpost before reaching the 32-mile mark on the route, the town of Morriston. You'll reach Morriston just after entering Levy County. There's a convenience store there, a couple of churches, a few houses and a Masonic lodge building.

You'll travel in Levy County for only about six miles before returning to Marion. Just before you turn from County Road 326 onto C.R. 225A, there will be another convenience store, then seven miles of some of the best horse farms in the area. This is rolling country, and the farms are immaculate with neat wooden fences and green pastures where the horses are being trained. Have your camera ready, because the picture-taking possibilities along this stretch of the route seem endless.

A few miles after leaving the horse farms, you'll turn onto C.R. 231. At this point there's a crossroads named Irvine. There's a large store here that's worth a stop. It sells antiques and Christmas decorations.

Irvine is only about five miles from the finish, so you'll have time to linger here. The next stop will be the little town of Orange Lake. It's on U.S. Highway 441 next to the lake with the same name. This is a popular fishing spot and one of the larger lakes in North Florida.

You will be on U.S. Highway 441 for less than two miles as you return to your starting point in McIntosh, but don't be alarmed by the divided four-lane highway. It's not that busy, and there's an extra lane for vehicles to pass you.

Once you're back in McIntosh, you may want to take a short ride around the town. It's an intriguing place that almost looks as if it's still in the 19th century. In the small business district there are a couple of interesting antiques stores.

McIntosh is a hilly town, but it's small enough that

you can pedal up and down all the streets in a short time. Once an outstanding produce and citrus center, the town now is largely populated by retirees or young couples raising families and commuting to jobs in Gainesville and Ocala.

The biggest event of the year is an 1890s festival that's held in October or November and attracts more than 40,000 visitors. There are tours of the Victorian homes, an arts and crafts show, a parade and a barbecue.

This is a delightful loop — rolling countryside, beautiful horse farms and a pleasant town at the start and finish. The distance easily can be negotiated in a single day even if you allow time to take pictures on the route and explore Irvine and McIntosh.

McIntosh-Morriston loop
1. Turn left out of Van Ness Park onto Avenue F and go one block to 8th Street.
2. Turn left on 8th Street and go one block to Avenue G.
3. Turn right on Avenue G and go one block to U.S. Highway 441.
4. Cross U. S. Highway 441 and go 6 miles to C.R. 329.
5. Turn left on C.R. 329 and go 8.3 miles to C.R. 225.
6. Turn right on C.R. 225 and go 7.6 miles to C.R. 326.
7. Turn right on C.R. 326 and go 9.2 miles to the intersection with C.R. 323.
8. Follow C.R. 326 to the left. Go one-half of a mile to junction of C.R. 326 and U.S. Highway 41 in town of Morriston.
9. Turn left on U.S. Highway 41 and go 2.3 miles to C.R. 464.
10. Turn left on C.R. 464 and go 9.5 miles to U.S. Highway 27.
11. Turn right on U.S. Highway 27 and go one-half of a mile to C.R. 225.

12. Turn left on C.R. 225 and go 3.2 miles to C.R. 326.
13. Turn right on C.R. 326 and go 3.9 miles to C.R. 225A.
14. Turn left on C.R. 225A and go 7 miles to C.R. 329.
15. Turn left on C.R. 329 and go three-tenths of a mile to C.R. 225.
16. Turn right on C.R. 225 and go 3.3 miles to C.R. 318.
17. Turn right on C.R. 318 and go 1.9 miles to N.W. 60 Avenue.
18. Turn left on N.W. 60 Avenue and go 1.3 miles to N.W. 191 Lane Road.
19. Turn right on N.W. 191 Lane Road and go two-tenths of a mile to U.S. Highway 441.
20. Turn left on U.S. Highway 441 and go 1.6 miles to Avenue F in McIntosh.
21. Turn right on Avenue F and return to starting point.

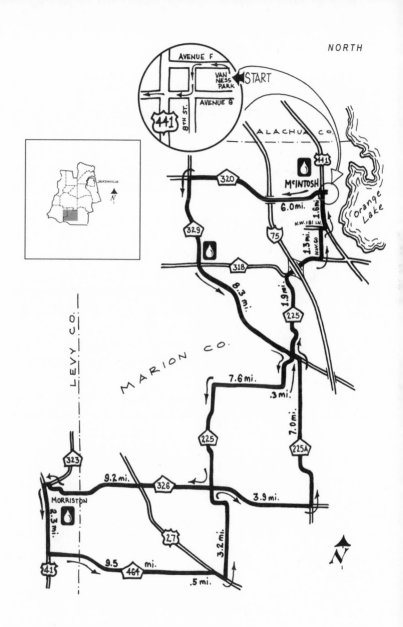

NORTH

AVENUE F

VAN NESS PARK

START

441

8TH ST.

AVENUE G

ALACHUA CO.

JACKSONVILLE

320

McINTOSH

441

6.0 mi.

1.6 mi.

Orange Lake

32.9

75

N.W. 191 LN.

1.3 mi.

N.W. 50

318

8.3 mi.

1.9 mi.

225

MARION CO.

LEVY CO.

7.6 mi.

.3 mi.

7.0 mi.

225

225A

323

9.2 mi.

326

3.9 mi.

MORRISTON

2.3 mi.

27

3.2 mi.

441

9.5 mi.

464

.5 mi.

N

103

▲ Orange Lake-Williston loop

You'll enjoy this 55-mile loop through the back roads of Marion and Levy counties.

This route starts in northern Marion County in the town of Orange Lake, which lies on the shores of one of North Florida's prime fishing areas, and then heads west through wooded country.

Just a few yards from your starting point at the Orange Lake post office where you can leave your car, you'll be on Dungarvin Road. Be prepared for some hill climbing. It's a roller coaster for five miles, but it's scenic country and you can coast down the hills.

Just before leaving County Road 320, you'll enter Levy County. The road narrows for the last half-mile before turning onto State Road 121. There are some rough spots on the seven-mile stretch of C.R. 335; portions of it are slag construction.

There will be about a mile on U.S. Highway 27-41 before you reach the town of Williston, but it's not too busy at this point. Williston will be your first chance to refuel since leaving Orange Lake. It's a town of about 2,500 with several restaurants and places for snacks and cold drinks. Fill your water bottles here because there won't be another chance to do so for about 15 miles.

The route follows U.S. Highway 27 for 2.4 miles when you leave Williston. Traffic moves slowly in town, but you'll have about a mile in open country before you return to another quiet country road.

You either will be in horse farm country or woods on the return route from Williston to Orange Lake. This area has become a prime horse breeding area in the United States in the last 35 years, ever since an exciting colt named Needles won the Kentucky Derby and the Belmont Stakes in 1956.

There were five horse farms in this area then; now there are more than 200. Needles was the first great Florida-bred horse, but there have been dozens of big winners since then.

Most of the horse farms are showplaces with miles of well-tended fences and acres of pastures where the animals are raised and trained for their performances on the nation's tracks.

A few miles from the finish you'll pass through Flemington. Though it is not a showplace, you may want to make a stop at the old-time country store at the junction of C.R. 318 and C.R. 329. It belongs to an earlier era, but it has managed to survive into the last decade of the 20th century. The old frame structure was unpainted for many years, but it's been brightened up with new paint recently. The interior is unchanged. Most crossroads like this now are served by modern convenience stores, so you may want to get a look at this Flemington relic. It's fully stocked with cold drinks and snacks. It's closed on Sunday.

From Flemington it's only a few more miles back to the starting point in Orange Lake. On C.R. 318, watch carefully for the road leading into Orange Lake. The usual county road marker has been replaced with a street sign like the type you'd find in town. It's marked N.W. 60 Ave. You also will see a 35-mph speed limit sign from C.R. 318. From that point, it's little more than a mile to Orange Lake.

There are several stores and places to get something to eat and drink at Orange Lake. This town is primarily interested in fishing, and the nearby lake draws fishermen from all over.

Aside from the horse farms, this area has remained virtually unchanged for many years. The roads are in good condition, and the traffic on most of the route is extremely light. The only rough road is C.R. 335 in Levy County, and the only real traffic is the mile on U.S. Highway 27 before you turn off onto C.R. 316.

Orange Lake-Williston loop

1. Turn left out of Orange Lake post office on single lane road, N.W. 193 Street, and go one block to Dungarvin Road, marked N.W. 192 Place.
2. Turn right on Dungarvin Road and go 5.2 miles to C.R. 329.
3. Turn right on C.R. 329 and go 2.1 miles to C.R. 320.
4. Turn left on C.R. 320 and go 6.8 miles to S.R. 121.
5. Turn left on S.R. 121 and go 2.3 miles to C.R. 335.
6. Turn right on C.R. 335 and go 7 miles to C.R. 241.
7. Turn left on C.R. 241 and go 1.5 miles to C.R. 343.
8. Turn left on C.R. 343 and go 4.2 miles to U.S. Highway 27-41.
9. Turn right on U.S. Highway 27-41 and go 1.1 miles to C.R. 318A.
10. Turn left on C.R. 318A and go eight-tenths of a mile to S.R. 121.

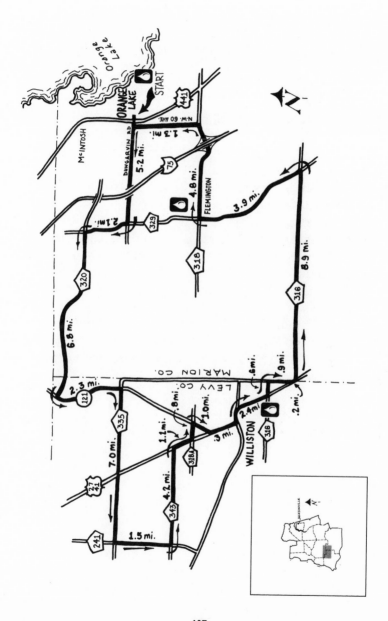

11. Turn right on S.R. 121 and go 1 mile to U.S. Highway 27-41.
12. Turn left on U.S. Highway 27-41 in Williston and go three-tenths of a mile to U.S. Highway 27.
13. Turn left on U.S. Highway 27 and go 2.4 miles to C.R. 316.
14. Turn left on C.R. 316 and go six-tenths of a mile to C.R. 335.
15. Turn right on C.R. 335 and go nine-tenths of a mile to U.S. Highway 27.
16. Turn left on U.S. Highway 27 and go two-tenths of a mile to C.R. 316.
17. Turn left on C.R. 316 and go 8.9 miles to C.R. 329.
18. Turn left on C.R. 329 and go 3.9 miles to C.R. 318.
19. Turn right on C.R. 318 and go 4.8 miles to unmarked road just before reaching U.S. Highway 441. Road has small street sign that marks it N.W. 60 Avenue.
20. Turn left on N.W. 60 Avenue and go 1.3 miles to Dungarvin Road, N.W. 192 Place.
21. Turn right on N.W. 192 Place and return to starting point at post office.

▲Paynes Prairie-Ocala National Forest loop

This loop takes two or three days, but it gives you the best possible look at the Ocala National Forest and other areas of Florida's outstanding natural beauty.

The route is about 183 miles long, starts and finishes at Paynes Prairie south of Gainesville and offers a variety of accommodations for overnight stops.

Of the three national forests in Florida, the Ocala National Forest is Central Florida's largest. This route exposes you to beautiful scenery and takes you the entire length of the forest from north to south.

In addition to exploring the national forest, the route also will take you through the scenic community of Cross Creek and past the little cottage where Marjorie Kinnan Rawlings wrote *The Yearling* and other well-known books about this backwoods part of Florida.

Before the route ends, you'll ride through the historic town of Micanopy.

If you're used to long distances on a bicycle, the route can be handled in two days, but to really savor the surroundings it is recommended you take three days.

For those choosing the three-day route, the suggested overnight stopping points are Salt Springs and Silver Springs. The distance to the campground at Salt Springs is 56.5 miles. From there to Silver Springs is 78 miles, which leaves a final day's ride of about 49 miles.

Those determined to negotiate the entire distance in two days will have a choice of campgrounds at Alexander Springs or Lake Dorr, both operated by the National Forest Service. It's about 82 miles to Alexander Springs and 84 miles to Lake Dorr. Riders who want motel accommodations can leave the route in Altoona and ride a couple of miles south on State Road 19 to the town of

Marjorie Kinnan Rawlings home in Cross Creek

Umatilla.

For those not wanting to camp, there are other accommodations at Salt Springs and Silver Springs on the three-day route.

Paynes Prairie State Preserve is the best starting point. You can park your car there safely for $2 per night. There also are camping areas, restrooms, shower facilities and a nice lake for swimming.

There will be only a couple of miles on four-laned U.S. Highway 441 at the beginning of the route before you head into the wooded areas approaching Cross Creek. Don't worry about U.S. Highway 441; traffic is not heavy.

Cross Creek is a quiet little community in the woods, little-changed from what it was a half-century ago, when Rawlings wrote *The Yearling*. Her simple frame cottage also is unchanged and is open to the public from 10 a.m. to 11:30 a.m. and 1 p.m. to 4:30 p.m. daily except Tuesday and Wednesday. Tours are conducted every half-hour, and each tour is limited to 10 persons. Rawlings did her writing and won a Pulitzer Prize in literature in a house without electricity, a telephone or running water.

From Cross Creek there will be more wooded areas on lightly traveled roads until you reach the Ocala National Forest. When you turn onto U.S. Highway 301 from County Road 325 there's a grocery store at the little town of Island Grove. That's at the 16-mile mark on the route. Traffic is fairly heavy and fast-moving on C.R. 301, but it's a divided four-lane road and you'll have only 2.6 miles of it. You'll leave C.R. 301 at the town of Citra, where there also is a grocery store. There also are grocery and convenience stores in Fort McCoy, 40 miles from the starting point.

From Fort McCoy to Salt Springs, your first overnight stop, it's a little more than 15 miles. The National Forest Service operates an excellent campground there with all the necessary facilities, including an outstanding swimming spot in the springs. These springs gush 52 million gallons of water daily, and the temperature is always 72 degrees. A restaurant, grocery and coin-operated laundry are nearby.

After leaving Salt Springs, it's more than 31 miles south on S.R. 19 until you turn west at Altoona on S.R. 42. There's some traffic on S.R. 19, but there's also a wide paved lane on both sides of the road for bicycles. You'll be in the forest the entire time and will enjoy riding through unspoiled country with large stands of pine and oak.

Be careful during the 11 miles on C.R. 42 west of Altoona. It's not heavy traffic, but the terrain is slightly rolling and there are several curves that make it hard for motorists to spot bicyclists from a distance.

The route turns north on Forest Road 8. Be alert; the road is not well-marked. Turn right at the convenience store named the Buck and Doe.

At about the 60-mile mark on your second day, you'll ride for less than two miles on S.R. 40. This is a busy road, but there's a bicycle lane. Except for that brief stretch, you'll ride the rest of this day in wooded country with little traffic.

Use caution in crossing S.R. 40 while riding on C.R. 314. It's about eight miles from there to the overnight stop at Silver Springs.

At Silver Springs you can choose between the Silver Springs Campers Garden or the Sun Plaza Motel. Both are well-recommended and are right across the street from the entrance to the well-known tourist attraction. Fees are reasonable.

It's a short distance to C.R. 35, the road you finished on yesterday. Continue north on that and back into the same kind of wilderness country you've experienced during the first two days of the ride.

From Fort McCoy the route turns west on C.R. 316. Be careful in crossing U.S. highways 301 and 441. They are four-lane roads with fast-moving traffic. You'll ride through the little town of Reddick and the community of Fairfield before turning onto C.R. 329 and the final miles of the trip.

County Road 329 becomes C.R. 234 when it enters Alachua County, then it's only a short distance from there until you enter Micanopy. The oldest inland town in Florida, Micanopy has a long history. Plan to spend some time browsing through the many antiques shops on the town's only business street and examining the various historical markers. The population is only a little more than 700. You'll want to ride your bike through the residential streets. There are trees everywhere, so the town is always shady.

It's less than two miles from here back to the starting point in Paynes Prairie. Be sure to stop at the visitor center before leaving. There are exhibits on the natural and cultural history of the preserve and an audio-visual program that tells how the resource management practices were used to preserve the basin's natural landscape. In the early days of Micanopy, Paynes Prairie was a lake and was used for shipping produce by barge to the railroad.

This scenic, interesting route winds through some of the state's most beautiful areas and highlights interesting little towns and communities that are off the beaten path and seldom visited by tourists. The roads are good, and the traffic rarely poses a problem.

Paynes Prairie-Ocala National Forest loop

1. Turn left from entrance to Paynes Prairie State Preserve onto U.S. Highway 441 and go 2.2 miles to C.R. 346.
2. Turn left on C.R. 346 and go 5.2 miles to C.R. 325.
3. Turn right on C.R. 325 and go 8.2 miles to U.S. Highway 301 in town of Island Grove.
4. Turn right on U.S. Highway 301 and go 2.6 miles to C.R. 318 in town of Citra.
5. Turn left on C.R. 318 and go 12.7 miles to C.R. 315 in town of Orange Springs.
6. Turn right on C.R. 315 and go 10 miles to C.R. 316 in town of Fort McCoy.
7. Turn left on C.R. 316 and go 15.5 miles to S.R. 19 and Salt Springs Recreation Area.
8. Turn right on S.R. 19 and go 31.5 miles to S.R. 42 in town of Altoona.
9. Turn right on C.R. 42 and go 11 miles to Forest Road 8.
10. Turn right on Forest Road 8 and go 7.9 miles to C.R.314A.
11. Turn left on C.R. 314A and go 10 miles to S.R. 40.

12. Turn left on S.R. 40 and go 1.6 miles to unmarked road at convenience store.
13. Turn right on unmarked road and go 4.9 miles to C.R. 314.
14. Turn left on C.R. 314 and go 2.6 miles to S.R. 40.
15. Cross S.R. 40 and continue on C.R. 314 for 6.7 miles to C.R. 35.
16. Turn right on C.R. 35 and go 1.7 miles to S.R. 40 and Silver Springs.
17. Cross S.R. 40 and continue on C.R. 35 for 5 miles to where road ends.
18. Turn right where road ends and go 4.5 miles to C.R. 315.
19. Turn left on C.R. 315 and go 6.1 miles to C.R. 316 and town of Fort McCoy.
20. Turn left on C.R. 316 and go 9.4 miles to C.R. 200A.
21. Turn right on C.R. 200A and go one-half of a mile to C. R. 316.
22. Turn left on C.R. 316 and go 9 miles to C.R. 329.
23. Turn right on C.R. 329 and go 12.5 miles to C.R. 25A and U.S. Highway 441 in town of Micanopy. C.R. 329 becomes C.R. 234 when it enters Alachua County.
24. Turn left on 25A and U.S. Highway 441 and go one-half of a mile to U.S. Highway 441 at north end of Micanopy.
25. Turn left on U. S. Highway 441 and go 1.3 miles to starting point at entrance to Paynes Prairie State Preserve.

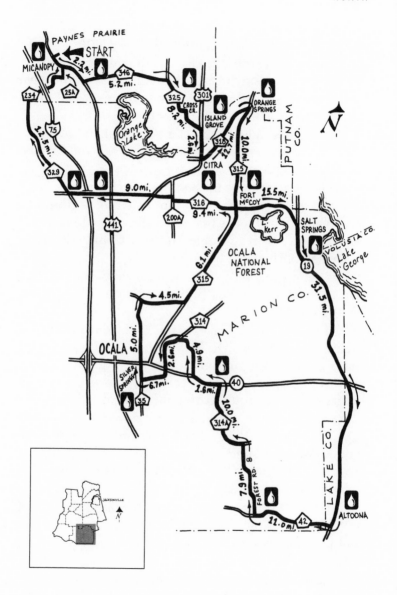

▲*Paynes Prairie-Salt Springs Highway loop*

If you want to tour the Ocala National Forest and the Marjorie Kinnan Rawlings home in Cross Creek and have only two days to ride, this 133-mile route cuts 50 miles off the three-day trip discussed earlier.

The route still lets you get a good look at the forest, enjoy the backwoods charm of Cross Creek and the historic town of Micanopy.

This route replaces the 30-mile stretch on State Road 19 that cuts through the forest for its entire north-south length and the 40 miles that wind through Altoona and Silver Springs with a 20-mile stretch on County Road 314 — the Salt Springs Highway.

To get acquainted with this tour, check the description of the longer route. It gives complete details of the highlights of the ride.

Cover the first 56.5 miles of this route from the Paynes Prairie State Preserve to Salt Springs, and then either camp at the campground run by the National Forest Service in Salt Springs or check in at one of the nearby lodges or motels. Your second day will cover 76.6 miles.

If you prefer to put in a longer day at the start and have more time at the end of the second day, ride from Paynes Prairie State Preserve to Silver Springs. If you cover that distance of 84.3 miles, it would leave only 48.8 miles on the second day.

At Silver Springs, choose either the Sun Plaza Motel or the Silver Springs Campers Garden for your overnight stay. Both places are just across the street from the tourist attraction.

There are advantages to stopping either at Salt Springs or Silver Springs. If you opt for the shorter ride on the first day, you'll be spending the night in an outstanding campground with all the facilities and a swimming spot that is hard to beat. By going the longer distance on the first day, you'll have more time to browse around the antiques shops and stroll the shaded streets of Micanopy at the end of the second day.

County Road 314 starts at the south end of Lake Kerr, the largest lake in the Ocala National Forest, and heads southwest through wooded country that is slightly rolling in spots. The road is good, and there's little traffic. This road is not on the longer route.

Paynes Prairie-Salt Springs Highway loop

1. Turn left at entrance to Paynes Prairie State Preserve onto U.S. Highway 441 and go 2.2 miles to C.R. 346.
2. Turn left on C.R. 346 and go 5.2 miles to C.R. 325.
3. Turn right on C.R. 325 and go 8.2 miles to U.S. Highway 301 in the town of Island Grove.
4. Turn right on U.S. Highway 301 and go 2.6 miles to C.R. 318 in town of Citra.
5. Turn left on C.R. 318 and go 12.7 miles to C.R. 315 in town of Orange Springs.
6. Turn right on C.R. 315 and go 10 miles to C.R. 316 in town of Fort McCoy.
7. Turn left on C.R. 316 and go 15.5 miles to S.R. 19 and Salt Springs Recreation Area.
8. Turn right on S.R. 19 and go nine-tenths of a mile to C.R. 314.
9. Turn right on C.R. 314 and go 18.5 miles to S.R 40.
10. Cross S.R. 40 and continue on C.R. 314 for 6.7 miles to C.R. 35.
11. Turn right on C.R. 35 and go 1.7 miles to S.R 40.
12. Cross S.R. 40 and continue on C.R. 35 for 5 miles to where road dead ends.
13. Turn right and go 4.5 miles to C.R. 315.
14. Turn left on C.R. 315 and go 6.1 miles to C.R. 316

and town of Fort McCoy.

15. Turn left on C.R. 316 and go 9.4 miles to C.R. 200A.
16. Turn right on C.R. 200A and go one-half of a mile to C.R. 316.
17. Turn left on C.R. 316 and go 9 miles to C.R. 329.
18. Turn right on C.R. 329 and go 12.5 miles to C.R. 25A and U.S. Highway 441 in town of Micanopy. C.R. 329 becomes C.R. 234 when it enters Alachua County.
19. Turn left on C.R. 25A and U.S. Highway 441 and go one-half of a mile to U.S. Highway 441 at north end of Micanopy.
20. Turn left on U.S. Highway 441 and go 1.3 miles to starting point at entrance to Paynes Prairie State Preserve.

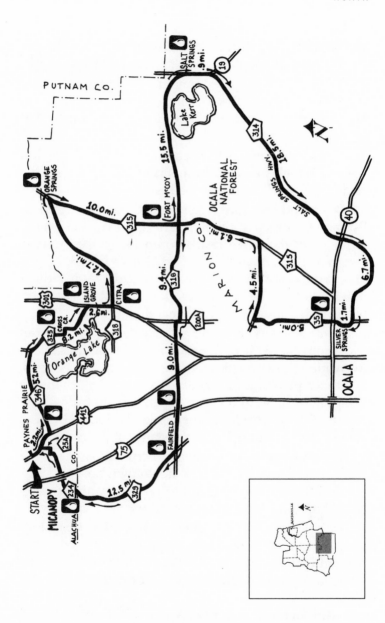

▲ Fort Clinch-Kingsley Plantation loop

This 51-mile route through Duval and Nassau counties loops through the extreme northeast corner of the state. The tour includes a visit to the oldest plantation house in Florida and a military fort that is almost 150 years old.

While the route easily can be handled in a single day, there's enough involved in this ride to warrant setting aside a full weekend to see it all.

Begin and end your ride in Fort Clinch State Park in Fernandina Beach at the northern tip of Amelia Island. From there the route heads south along the Atlantic Ocean on State Road A1A to Fort George Island. After a visit to the historic Kingsley Plantation, the route returns to S.R. A1A for several miles, then it turns inland and brings you into downtown Fernandina Beach.

If you want to make this a single day's ride, you can leave your car in the parking lot of the Fernandina Beach Recreation Department across the street from Fort Clinch. For those planning to make a weekend of it, there are camping facilities at the fort, which is open from 8 a.m. to sunset daily. There are several motels along S.R. A1A, some of them within walking distance of the fort.

A visit to the restored area of Fernandina Beach is a must on this trip. A 30-block downtown area was restored in the 1970s to its turn-of-the-century appearance. Nice shops and good restaurants draw tourists daily.

In Florida, only St. Augustine has a longer history than Fernandina Beach. The Spanish established a post there in 1686, and the city has the distinction of being the only place in the United States to have existed under eight flags.

Another highlight in Fernandina's history came in

Fort Clinch

the 1850s when David Levy Yulee built the state's first cross-state railroad from Fernandina to Cedar Key.

Be sure to visit the Palace Saloon on your tour of the restored area. It has been there since 1903, giving it the distinction of being the oldest saloon in Florida still in its original location. Featured there is a huge hand-carved mahogany bar, a tin ceiling and murals painted in 1907.

The Amelia Island Museum in the downtown area is open Monday through Saturday and provides an interesting look at the history of the area. Even if you don't stay at Fort Clinch, you'll want to ride your bike through it and spend some time exploring the fort. There's a small admission fee.

Though the fort is the major attraction in the park, the 1,086 acres include a nature trail through a coastal hammock and huge sand dunes along the east side of the park near the ocean. There's a wide beach area for swimming, a pier for fishing and three different areas for camping. Cumberland Sound is on the northern side of the park, just a short distance from Georgia.

Fort Clinch, a large and impressive structure overlooking Cumberland Sound, was built before the Civil War. Records are sketchy, but construction was believed to have started in 1847. The fort was named in honor of Gen. Duncan Clinch, who fought in the Second Seminole War.

When the Civil War began, the fort was only partially finished. The Confederates captured it in 1861 without Federal resistance. By early the next year, several coastal islands had been captured. Fernandina was isolated. Gen. Robert E. Lee authorized the Confederates to leave the fort, allowing a Union takeover.

New cannon designs later made the fort obsolete, and it was deactivated in 1867. It was used briefly during the Spanish-American War but finally offered for sale by the federal government in 1926 and purchased by Florida in 1936.

The last time the fort was used in service was during World War II, when the Coast Guard maintained a surveillance system on the coastal islands in the area.

Men from the Civilian Conservation Corps did most of the restoration work from 1937 to 1942. Walking through this fort now is like stepping back to the Civil War era.

From the fort the route heads for S.R. A1A, which hugs the coast for more than five miles before turning inland. Before you reach Fort George Island, you'll pass Little Talbot Island State Park. This is one of a chain of unique islands off the northeast coast. Little Talbot encompasses about 2,500 acres of land. Wind and sea have changed its size and shape over the years. Swimmers are attracted to the island by the long and wide stretch of beach. Campgrounds with full facilities are in the wooded areas across S.R. A1A. From Little Talbot it's

Fort Clinch

about five miles to the road that turns off S.R. A1A toward the Kingsley Plantation.

When you make the turn you'll see an old two-story frame house on your left. That was the home of Napoleon Broward, governor of Florida from 1905 to 1909 and the man Broward County was named after. Members of the Broward family still are living there.

As you pedal toward the Kingsley Plantation, you'll see a sign on your left pointing toward the plantation. Don't take the road — two miles of sand make it rough going! Continue on the paved road and go through the Fort George Island Country Club. About nine-tenths of a mile from the plantation the road turns to dirt, but it's well-packed and you should be able to ride in from there.

Just before you reach the plantation, you'll pass a row of abandoned buildings. These are the remaining outside walls of the slave cabins. There were 32 originally; 24 are left. They were built of tabby, a primitive type of concrete made of sand, oyster shell and water.

The plantation grounds are open from 8 a.m. to sunset

Kingsley Plantation House

daily, and guided tours are provided for a small fee at 9:30 a.m., 11 a.m., 1:30 p.m. and 3 p.m.

The tour includes a trip through the house with interesting details about the Kingsley family and the fascinating history of the plantation.

The Kingsley Plantation is one of the few remaining examples of the plantation system of territorial Florida and is the site of the oldest plantation house in the state. The building in which the visitor center is located was reportedly built in 1791 by John McQueen, who received the island from the king of Spain.

The island became the property of Zephaniah Kingsley in 1817, when he purchased it for $7,000 from John Houstoun McIntosh. Kingsley built the plantation house that same year and continued to manage the island until 1840. He was appointed to the second Legislative Council of the Florida territory by President James Monroe and became a wealthy landowner. He also had a large number of slaves. On a trip to Madagascar he married a 12-year-old Negro princess named Anna Madegigine Jai and brought her back to the plantation. He complied with convention by having her live in one house while he lived in the main house.

Sea-island cotton, corn and sugar cane were the primary crops grown on the island.

Kingsley died in 1843 in his sister's home in New York. This sister was Martha Kingsley McNeill, who was the grandmother of James McNeill Whistler, the famous artist.

As you leave the road to the plantation to return to S.R. A1A, there will be a marker on your right. Jean Ribault and a party of Huguenots landed near here on May 1, 1562, and knelt in prayer. This was supposed to have been the first Protestant prayer in North America.

The return route will take you back to Fernandina Beach. If you missed touring the restored downtown area earlier, you can catch it now before returning to Fort Clinch and the end of the route.

If it's a hot day, the public beach is nearby off S.R. A1A. The ride along S.R. A1A is one of the prettiest in Florida and offers a wide range of scenery. This, coupled with the two historical sites and the restored area of Fernandina Beach, makes this loop a memorable experience.

Fort Clinch-Kingsley Plantation loop

1. Exit left out of entrance to Fort Clinch on Atlantic Avenue and go one-tenth of a mile to S.R. A1A.
2. Turn right on S.R. A1A and go 5.8 miles to a flashing red light.
3. Turn left at the light and go 15.8 miles to Fort George Road.
4. Turn right on Fort George Road leading into Kingsley Plantation and go 2.3 miles to where the

paving ends.

5. Continue on the dirt road for seven-tenths of a mile to a turn in the road.

6. Turn right on the dirt road and go through the old slave quarters for two-tenths of a mile to the parking lot for the plantation.

7. Exit on the same dirt road and follow it for two-tenths of a mile to left turn in road.

8. Turn left and go seven-tenths of a mile to where paving resumes.

9. Go straight ahead on paving for 2.3 miles to S.R. A1A.

10. Turn left on S.R. A1A and go 15.8 miles to a flashing yellow light.

11. Go straight ahead at flashing light onto C.R. 105A and go 2 miles to 14th Street.

12. Turn right on 14th Street and go 3.6 miles to Atlantic Avenue in Fernandina Beach.

13. Turn right on Atlantic Avenue and go 1.2 miles to Fort Clinch and end of route.

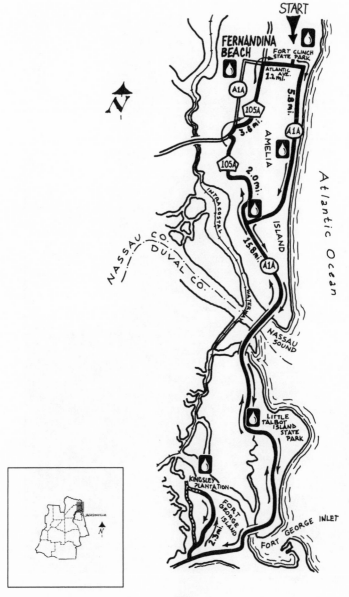

START

FERNANDINA
BEACH
FORT CLINCH
STATE PARK

ATLANTIC
AVE.
2.2 mi.

A1A

105A

3.8 mi.

5.8 mi.

AMELIA

A1A

105A

2.0 mi.

15.8 mi.

ISLAND

A1A

NASSAU CO.
DUVAL CO.

INTRACOSTAL

WATERWAY

NASSAU
SOUND

Atlantic Ocean

LITTLE
TALBOT
ISLAND
STATE
PARK

KINGSLEY
PLANTATION

FORT
GEORGE
ISLAND

FORT GEORGE INLET

2.3 mi.

JACKSONVILLE

127

Castillo De San Marcos

▲ Palatka-St. Augustine loop

This 83-mile route includes a visit to St. Augustine, the oldest city in the United States. It passes hundreds of acres of potatoes and cabbages and can be ridden either in one or two days, depending on how much time you spend in St. Augustine.

For those who want to sightsee in St. Augustine, leave your car in Palatka, spend the night at a motel or campground in St. Augustine and return the next day to Palatka.

The distance from Palatka to St. Augustine is 46 miles; the return trip, over a different route, is 37 miles.

There is plenty of good scenery on this route — you'll ride along the wide St. Johns River, pass by thick woods and travel through hundreds of acres of potato and cabbage fields.

You may park your car overnight in a lot across the street from the Palatka police station. It's well-lighted, and there are officers on duty throughout the night.

The first stop on the route will be less than two miles from the starting point when you turn into Ravine Gardens. Created in 1933 by the Federal Works Project Administration, the gardens were maintained by the city of Palatka until 1970, when they became part of the Florida state park system.

These gardens are a dramatic example of the way water has shaped the land. The steep ravine in the gardens was created by water flowing under sandy ridges that flank the west shore of the St. Johns River. The slopes of the ravine gradually were colonized by grasses and shrubs that slowed the erosion process. Trees eventually became established and created the mixed hardwood forest that is there now.

The best time of the year for seeing the gardens is in March and April when the azaleas and camellias are blooming.

There's a 1.8-mile one-way loop road for viewing the ravine from your bike, and there also are walking trails which lead around the ravine and along the spring-fed creek.

From the gardens the route proceeds on River Street along the St. Johns River. Many stately old homes are on this street, and in a few more blocks you'll be on the main business street of Palatka heading up the high bridge that crosses the St. Johns River.

Palatka and the rest of Putnam County bill themselves as the Bass Capital of the World. Fishermen from all over descend on the area to haul large bass from the St. Johns and the small lakes scattered about the county. The river is wide at this point, and there always are fishing boats in search of those bass.

The potato and cabbage fields are in evidence as soon as you leave East Palatka and enter the rural areas. These fields end abruptly when the route turns onto County Road 13, the William Bartram Scenic Highway. This road parallels the St. Johns River for several miles. It's a beautiful stretch of road with the wide river on one side and thick woods on the other.

After about 10 miles the route turns east toward St. Augustine. Now there are more fields of potatoes and cabbages, and the only relief is a little convenience store at a place with the somewhat unusual name of Molasses Junction.

There are about 15 miles on C.R. 214 before reaching St. Augustine. This first day's ride ends at the parking lot outside the Visitor Information Center, right across the street from the famous Castillo de San Marcos. Spaniards

The Bridge of Lions

built this fortress in the 17th century.

A tour of the fortress takes about an hour. After that there is still quite a bit to see in this city that has been around since 1565. Most sights are concentrated in the downtown area within walking distance.

For those spending the night in St. Augustine, the Visitor Information Center can supply information about motel and campground facilities as well as restaurants.

For swimmers, there's a good beach on the Atlantic across Matanzas Bay from St. Augustine. You'll need to cross the Bridge of Lions. Walk your bike across — the bridge is narrow with lots of traffic. Anastasia State Park also is located across the bridge. It has good camping facilities and beach access for swimming.

The return trip will take you along several of St. Augustine's narrow streets before you head onto U.S. Highway 1. This is a four-lane divided highway, but it's not very busy. Most of the north-south traffic is on Interstate 95 just a short distance away.

There will be five miles on U.S. Highway 1 before you turn west on C.R. 206. The only town before your return to Palatka will be Hastings, a quiet town with about 300 people. You'll be riding on the Cracker Swamp Road for six miles before rejoining civilization in Palatka.

Your ride through Hastings will be the second of the trip, since you visited the town before turning onto the scenic route along the St. Johns River on your ride to St. Augustine.

This is an easy loop with good roads, little traffic and enough scenery to make it interesting. Though the ride between the two cities is not long either day, keep in mind that the watering stops are few; make sure your water bottles are full before you leave.

Palatka-St. Augustine loop
1. Turn left out of parking lot on 11th Street to St. Johns Avenue.
2. Turn right on St. Johns Avenue and go six-tenths of a mile to Moseley Avenue.
3. Turn left on Moseley Avenue and go eight-tenths of a mile to Twigg Street.
4. Turn left on Twigg Street and go two-tenths of a mile to Ravine Gardens.
5. Turn right into Ravine Gardens.
6. Turn right after leaving Ravine Gardens and go one-tenth of a mile to 15th Street.
7. Turn left on 15th Street and go a few yards to River Street.
8. Turn right on River Street and go 1.1 miles to Laurel Street.
9. Turn right on Laurel Street and go one-tenth of a mile to South 2nd Street.
10. Turn left on South 2nd Street and go one-tenth of a mile to U.S. Highway 17, Reid Street.
11. Turn right on U.S. Highway 17 and go 1.4 miles to Masters Street.
12. Turn left on Masters Street and go two-tenths of a mile to Ferry Road.
13. Turn right on Ferry Road and go one-half of a mile to Putnam County Boulevard.
14. Turn left at stop sign onto Putnam County Boulevard and go 2.9 miles to C.R. 207A.
15. Turn right on C.R. 207A and go 2.9 miles to Federal Point Road.
16. Turn left on Federal Point Road and go 1.8 miles to Old Hastings Road just after small bridge.
17. Turn right on Old Hastings Road and go nine-tenths of a mile to County Line Road.
18. Turn left on County Line Road and go 1 mile to

Federal Point Road.

19. Turn right on Federal Point Road and go eight-tenths of a mile to Main Street in Hastings.
20. Turn right on Main Street in Hastings and go one-tenth of a mile to St. Johns Avenue. After crossing railroad tracks, St. Johns Avenue becomes C.R. 13.
21. Turn left on St. Johns Avenue and go 1.3 miles to C.R. 207.
22. Turn left on C.R. 207 and go 1.7 miles to C.R. 13 which also is William Bartram Scenic Highway.
23. Turn left on C.R. 13 and go 10.4 miles to C.R. 214.
24. Turn right on C.R. 214, which becomes King Street in St. Augustine, and go 15.6 miles to Riberia Street after crossing U. S. Highway 1.
25. Turn left on Riberia Street and go six-tenths of a mile to Castillo Drive.
26. Turn right on Castillo Drive and go two-tenths of a mile to Visitor Information Center parking lot at corner of Castillo Drive and San Marco Avenue. Suggested stopping point for night is St. Augustine.
27. Turn left out of parking lot onto Castillo Drive and go two-tenths of a mile to Riberia Street.
28. Turn left on Riberia Street and go six-tenths of a mile to King Street.
29. Turn right on King Street and go six-tenths of a mile to Leonardi Street. No sign for Leonardi Street, but St. Augustine Glass & Supply Co. is on the left.
30. Turn left on Leonardi Street, which becomes South Dixie Highway and C.R. 5A, and go 4.5 miles to U.S. Highway 1.
31. Turn right on U.S. Highway 1 and go 5.2 miles to State Road 206.
32. Turn right on S.R. 206 and go 10.8 miles to C.R. 207.
33. Turn left on C.R. 207 and go one-half of a mile to C.R. 13.

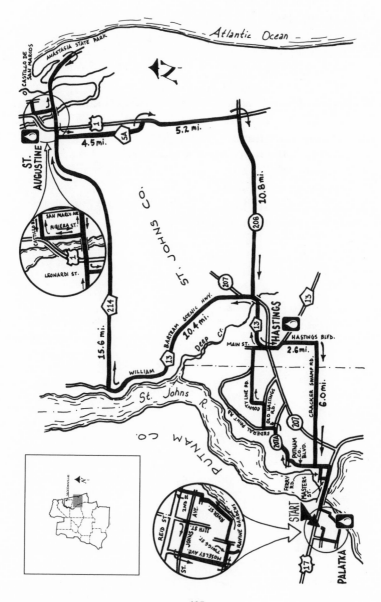

34. Turn right on C.R. 13 and go 1.2 miles to Main Street in Hastings.
35. Turn left on Main Street after stop sign and go 1.2 miles to Hastings Boulevard.
36. Turn right on Hastings Boulevard and go 2.6 miles to Cracker Swamp Road.
37. Turn right on Cracker Swamp Road and go 6 miles to Putnam County Boulevard in East Palatka.
38. Turn left on Putnam County Boulevard and go 1.3 miles to U.S. Highway 17, Reid Street.
39. Turn right on U.S. Highway 17 and go 2.6 miles to 11th Street in Palatka.
40. Turn left on 11th Street and return to parking lot across street from police station.

▲ *St. Augustine-Ponte Vedra Beach loop*

A ride of more than 20 miles along the Atlantic coast and a tour of the oldest city in the United States are included in a loop that begins and ends in St. Augustine.

The 56-mile loop easily can be handled in a day, and you'll have time for exploring the Atlantic beaches as well as historic St. Augustine. But many cyclists will want to spend an extra day here to enjoy browsing around the fascinating city.

According to historians it was here that Juan Ponce de Leon landed in 1513 in search of the legendary Fountain of Youth. The first permanent European settlement in the United States was established in St. Augustine in 1565 by Pedro Menendez de Aviles.

In the years that followed, the city was sacked by pirates in the 16th and 17th centuries.

While St. Augustine was under Spanish control in its early years, the English began extending their holdings southward. Spain responded by building Castillo de San Marcos in 1672. This impressive fortress still is intact and is open to the public. A small fee is charged. If you haven't visited the fort, make it a point to stop here for at least an hour. Located on Matanzas Bay, the fort affords an excellent view of the Atlantic. It has experienced a long and colorful history during its more than 300 years, and exhibits on display there make it a worthwhile visit.

If you start your ride from the Visitor Information Center on the corner of Castillo Drive and San Marco Avenue and leave your car there, you'll be just a short walk from the Castillo de San Marcos. Also nearby is the restored Spanish Quarter, an interesting collection of small shops. The oldest wooden schoolhouse in the United States is among the shops.

The Oldest House, St. Augustine

Your tour of St. Augustine may come either before or after the bike ride, which is highlighted by a long ride along the Atlantic's edge.

Just after leaving the Visitor Information Center, you'll turn onto U.S. Highway 1. It's a four-lane divided highway, but the traffic is not heavy. After leaving St. Augustine this traffic becomes even lighter, and it's a ride of 16 miles to County Road 210. While the entire loop is within St. Johns County, you'll be only two miles from Duval County when you reach the northernmost point of the loop and turn onto C.R. 203.

From the time you reach C.R. 203 until you head inland in St. Augustine for more than 20 miles, you're seldom out of sight of the Atlantic. This is a great stretch for biking with a good road, light traffic and miles and miles of sand dunes. There are dozens of expensive homes along here, but some areas have not been developed, and it's easy to reach the ocean. Just walk over the sand dunes, and it will be only a few feet to the beach. If you're riding on a hot day, any spot along C.R. 203 or

State Road A1A is ideal for a swim or just wading in the surf.

With so much development along the Atlantic coast of Florida over the years, this is probably the longest stretch of highway in the state that is right next to the ocean and so free of traffic. The further south you travel in Florida the more congested it becomes and the tougher it is to enjoy riding a bicycle.

The route turns westward just as you near St. Augustine. There's a drawbridge over the Matanzas River (the Intracoastal Waterway), and you're in St. Augustine.

Your last mile of the loop will take you down San Marco Avenue, which is also U.S. Business 1 and S.R. A1A.

There are no traffic problems on this loop, and the ride down S.R. A1A and C.R. 203 makes it a real delight. The ride on C.R. 10A just before you reach C.R. 203 is alongside the Intracoastal Waterway and very scenic. This is followed by about a mile through the residential areas of Ponte Vedra Beach before reaching the ocean.

Be sure you stock up on water before leaving. There's a convenience store on S.R. A1A, but it's 45 miles from your starting point. You may want to have a couple of extra bottles of water in your handlebar bag, especially if it's a hot day.

If you're interested in accommodations for the night when you finish your ride, there are several motels within a short distance of the Visitor Center. Plenty of good restaurants also are within easy walking distance. St. Augustine is not a difficult town to find your way around in, even though much of it was laid out centuries ago. If you do have questions, the Visitor Center has all the answers.

St. Augustine-Ponte Vedra Beach loop

1. Turn left out of parking lot at Visitor Center on Castillo Drive and go three-tenths of a mile to U. S. Highway 1.
2. Turn right on U.S. Highway 1 and go 16 miles to C.R. 210.
3. Turn right on C.R. 210 and go 5.8 miles to C.R. 210A.
4. Turn left on C.R. 210A and go 8.5 miles to C.R. 203. C.R. 210A becomes Solano Road after crossing S.R. A1A.
5. Turn right on C.R. 203 and go 5.1 miles to S.R. A1A.
6. Turn left on S.R. A1A and go 19.4 miles to intersection with U.S. Business 1 in St. Augustine. It's also S. R. A1A.
7. Turn left on U. S. Business 1 and go eight-tenths of a mile to parking lot at Visitor Center.

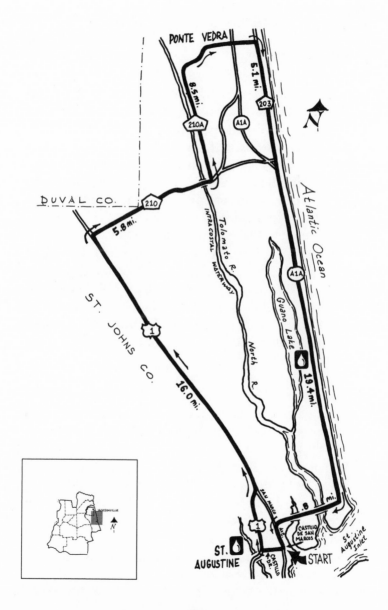

PONTE VEDRA

5.1 mi.

8.5 mi.

210A

A1A

203

N

Atlantic Ocean

DUVAL CO.

210

5.8 mi.

Tolomato R.

INTRACOSTAL WATERWAY

A1A

Guano Lake

ST. JOHNS CO.

1

16.0 mi.

North R.

19.4 mi.

JACKSONVILLE

N

.8 mi.

SAN MARCO AVE

CASTILLO DE SAN MARCOS

St. Augustine Inlet

ST. AUGUSTINE

1

CASTILLO DR.

START

▲ Bronson-Yankeetown loop

Here's a foray into the back roads of Levy County that leads to one of Florida's most isolated towns. This 86-mile ride can be handled either as a one-day trip or a weekend outing. It starts and ends in Bronson; the suggested overnight stop is in Yankeetown.

Start this ride at the post office in Bronson on U.S. Highway 27A. Bronson, Levy County's county seat, is one of the state's smallest with a population of about 700. If you're planning to make this a two-day trip, you may want to check with the sheriff's office at the courthouse about leaving your car near there. Park at the post office if you're going to make the loop in a single day.

After leaving Bronson on County Road 337 you'll quickly find yourself in rural, heavily wooded country. There's very little traffic on County Road 337. At the 11.5-mile mark, you'll cross C.R. 326; there's a convenience store at the intersection. The road for the next six miles, will be slag construction, but it's not as rough as most roads of this type.

After 22.6 miles, you reach U.S. Highway 19-98, a four-lane divided highway. Turn left. You'll be on this for more than eight miles, but the traffic isn't heavy and the extra lane gives cars and trucks plenty of room to get around you.

Watch closely for C.R. 40A. It's not marked on U.S. Highway 19-98, but it will be the first paved road on your right. This road will take you past the little settlement of Crackertown, apparently named to rival neighboring Yankeetown.

When you turn right off C.R. 40A onto C.R. 40 you'll be in Yankeetown. From there you'll have 3.6 more miles to the end of the route. The road parallels the Withlacoochee River and winds through salt marshes. It's a dramatic change in landscape before the road ends at the Gulf of Mexico. There's a little park there with picnic tables and restrooms. It's a popular fishing spot for snaring the great variety of fish in Withlacoochee Bay and the Gulf.

Backtrack to Yankeetown. It's a quaint town with about 600 residents tucked next to the Withlacoochee River. Woods are so thick here it looks as if the only trees that were removed were those that made room for the buildings.

Yankeetown was founded in 1923 by Judge A. F. Knotts of Gary, Ind. Knotts and his nephew set up a small fishing camp and a few houses and had plans to start a community. They called it Knotts, but Southerners nearby — in particular a rural mail carrier — resented the Yankee invasion and derisively called it Yankeetown. Two years later the town was incorporated, and the Yankeetown label stuck.

There's a post office, a town hall and a library but only a few retail businesses. A general store, a gas station, fishing camps, marinas and a rustic lodge make up the retail sector of Yankeetown. The Izaak Walton Lodge, originally built in 1924, was restored completely in 1987 and now is the showplace of Yankeetown. There are 10 rooms available complete with antique iron beds. Downstairs there's a 40-seat formal dining room. The lodge's restaurant, Izaak's Gourmet Restaurant, is correctly named. The meals are excellent, and the decor is pleasantly rustic. If you're going to spend the night, it's advisable to have advance reservations. Room prices are reasonable.

The return trip to Bronson takes you through the neighboring river town of Inglis, a place about double the size of Yankeetown. At this point you return to U.S. Highway 19-98 and pedal on it for more than 17 miles before heading into the hinterlands again on C.R. 326. The community of Gulf Hammock is located at this junction; there's a convenience store there.

Shortly after getting on C.R. 326 you'll come to the Henry Beck County Park. It's a good location to stop for a rest and a cold drink. There are restrooms here and picnic tables.

After turning off C.R. 326, you'll be back on C.R. 337, the road you took out of Bronson, for the final 11 miles of the loop.

Bronson has several places where you can get snacks and cold drinks as you finish your ride.

Levy County is located in the west central part of Florida. While it covers a large area, the trees outnumber the people. Wood products, quite naturally, account for a major portion of the economy. Despite the small population, the county has quite a labyrinth of hard-surfaced roads, mostly in the upper half. Most of the lower half is occupied by the Gulf Hammock Wildlife Management area. This is total wilderness with thousands of acres of woods and small streams. Yankeetown, Inglis and historic Cedar Key are the only towns in this half of the county.

If you like rides on very quiet roads that will put you in close touch with nature, you'll thoroughly enjoy this loop. The visit to Yankeetown and the marshlands around it make this a trip with considerable variety of terrain.

If you've managed to handle this loop in a single day, there's still another ride that is entirely within Levy County. It goes from Manatee Springs State Park, west of Chiefland, to Cedar Key and back.

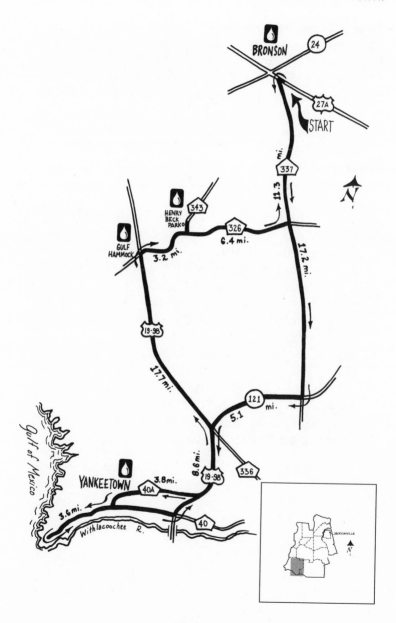

BRONSON

24

27A

START

337

11.3 mi.

NORTH

HENRY BECK PARK

343

326

6.4 mi.

GULF HAMMOCK

3.2 mi.

17.2 mi.

19-98

17.7 mi.

121

5.1 mi.

8.6 mi.

19-98

336

YANKEETOWN

3.8 mi.

40A

3.6 mi.

Withlacoochee R.

40

Gulf of Mexico

JACKSONVILLE

N

Bronson-Yankeetown loop

1. Turn left out of Bronson post office and go three-tenths of a mile on U.S. Highway 27A to C.R. 337.
2. Turn left on C.R. 337 and go 17.2 miles to S.R. 121.
3. Turn right on S.R. 121 and go 5.1 miles to U.S. Highway 19-98.
4. Turn left on U.S. Highway 19-98, crossing over northbound lane, and go 8.6 miles to C.R. 40A.
5. Turn right on C.R. 40A and go 3.8 miles to C.R. 40.
6. Turn right on C.R. 40 and go 3.6 miles to end of road.
7. Turn around on C.R. 40 and go 6.8 miles to U.S. Highway 19-98 staying on C.R. 40 when you come to junction with C.R. 40A.
8. Turn left on U.S. Highway 19-98 and go 17.7 miles to C.R. 326 at Gulf Hammock.
9. Turn right on C.R. 326 and go 3.2 miles to Henry Beck County Park on C.R. 343. Park is three-tenths of a mile from C.R. 326.
10. Return to C.R. 326 from park and go 6.4 miles to C.R. 337.
11. Turn left on C.R. 337 and go 11.3 miles to U.S. Highway 27A in Bronson.
12. Turn right on U.S. Highway 27A and go three-tenths of a mile back to starting point at post office.

▲*Gilchrist County loop*

Gilchrist County is among the least populated of Florida's 67 counties, so it's not surprising this 65-mile route is on quiet, lightly traveled roads.

Trenton, Gilchrist County's seat, is the starting and stopping point. A town with a population of about 1,200, Trenton is about 30 miles west of Gainesville on State Road 26.

Until 1925 Gilchrist County was part of Alachua County. A squabble over the lack of roads in the area that's now Gilchrist resulted in that part of Alachua seceding and establishing its own government. Named for Albert H. Gilchrist, a former governor of Florida, it was the last county in the state to be established.

Forming their own county didn't solve all Gilchrist County's problems. In a 1930 census, Gilchrist's population numbered over 4,000. The figures dwindled to only 2,868 in a 1960 census. With so few taxpayers, the county explored the possibility of consolidating with another county, but the decision was made to stick it out. This proved wise, for the 1980 census showed the population had doubled since 1960. Growth has continued since then.

Dairy farms and watermelons are the major agricultural pursuits in the county, and you'll see plenty of both on the route.

You'll pedal through the Waccasassa Flats, a marshy area occupying a large part of the county, shortly after leaving Trenton on S.R. 47.

Start the route at City Hall, a block north of S.R. 26 on Main Street in Trenton. There are plenty of parking spaces next to City Hall on the weekend. If you decide to ride on another day of the week, parking should not be a problem in other areas of the business section. The directions and mileage figures are from City Hall.

After Trenton you'll be riding in rural, unpopulated country. Much of the countryside is being used for farming, though there are some wooded areas. It's flat terrain throughout; you won't have to shift gears.

Two major Florida rivers — the Suwannee River on the west and the Sante Fe River on the north — serve as the boundaries for Gilchrist County. You'll visit Hart Springs, one of the county's six large springs. Hart Springs is a county park and is one of the best swimming spots in this part of Florida.

The roads in Gilchrist are good quality and well-marked, though advance warning of approaching turns sometimes is limited.

At the 15-mile mark on the route, there will be a gas station and store on your right at the junction of S.R. 47 and County Road 340. It serves sandwiches and cold drinks, but it's closed on Sunday. If you turn right on C.R. 340, you will be only two miles from a road leading into Ginnie Springs. This is not part of the route, but you may want to take a side trip. Ginnie Springs, on the Santa Fe River, is a beautiful spot for swimming, canoeing and scuba diving. It's a private campground with good facilities. There's an admission charge.

Just past that point on S.R. 47 (which you'll ride on for almost 18 miles), you suddenly turn onto C. R. 138 without warning. It's the third hard-surfaced road you'll see after leaving Trenton. There's a sign on the right that advertises Ginnie Springs.

After more than eight miles on C.R. 138, the route turns south on U.S. Highway 129. The traffic is very light.

When you turn onto C.R. 340 and head west, you're bound for the Suwannee River. The road turns south after

Fanning Springs

a short distance, but it's recommended you continue straight ahead. It's about a half-mile to the historic Suwannee River, where there's a little wayside park in a wooded section and the Rock Bluff General Store. This is a little past the halfway mark on the route, and it is a good place to stop for lunch and a good look at the river. Be forewarned — though swimming is permitted, alligators are spotted occasionally.

About 17 miles before the route ends, you'll reach Hart Springs. There are bathhouse facilities there, a concession stand and many sheltered picnic tables. It's an excellent place for a cool dip after more than 45 miles of pedaling.

From here the road makes several turns on its way back to Trenton. You'll be on S.R. 26 for a mile after skirting the little town of Fanning Springs. This is a fairly busy road, but you'll turn off it onto C.R. 341 after just one mile. Now it will be all rural roads back into Trenton.

When you reach the finish at City Hall, you'll be only a block from the only traffic light in Gilchrist County. In a state that's the fourth most populous in the United States, visitors find it hard to believe there's a county with only ONE traffic light. It gives you a pretty fair idea of how quiet a ride you will be experiencing as you tour the county that was the last in Florida to be formed, almost didn't make it a few years ago, and now has bounced back to a full recovery. It's a delightful county for touring.

If you want to include another day's tour on your weekend itinerary, there is another loop from Manatee Springs to Cedar Key and back. It starts near Chiefland, only 10 miles southwest of Trenton.

Gilchrist County loop

1. Turn right from Trenton City Hall and go three-tenths of a mile to S.R. 47.
2. Turn right on S.R. 47 and go 17.8 miles to C.R. 138.
3. Turn left on C.R. 138 and go 8.4 miles to U.S. Highway 129. C.R. 138 is unmarked on S.R. 47, but there's a sign for Ginnie Springs on right.
4. Turn left on U.S. Highway 129 and go 6.7 miles to C.R. 340.
5. Turn right on C.R. 340 and go 2.7 miles to where C.R. 340 turns left. If you go past the turn for one-half of a mile you'll be at Rock Bluff General Store and wayside park on Suwannee River.
6. Return to where C.R. 340 turns south, turn right and go 7.2 miles to C.R. 232.
7. Turn right on C.R. 232 and go 1 mile to where C.R. 232 turns left.
8. Turn left on C.R. 232 and go 1.4 miles to C.R. 344.
9. Turn right on C.R. 344 and go 1.7 miles to Hart Springs.
10. Turn right into Hart Springs and go two-tenths of a mile to parking lot. Return on same road to C.R. 344.
11. Turn left on C.R. 344 and go 1.7 miles to C.R. 232.

NORTH

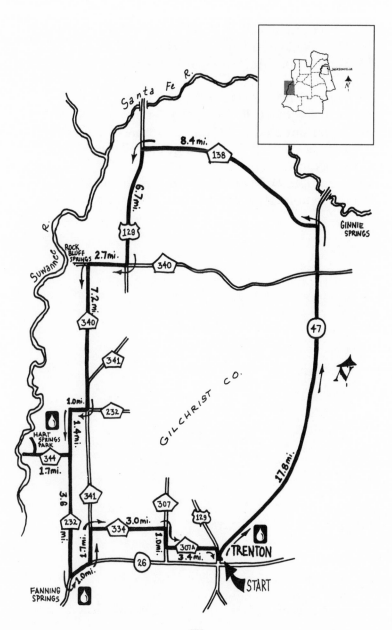

151

12. Turn right on C.R. 232 and go 3.6 miles to stop sign and S.R. 26 near Fanning Springs.
13. Turn left on S.R. 26 and go 1 mile to C.R. 341. Gulf gas station on right.
14. Turn left on C.R. 341 and go 1.7 miles to C.R. 334.
15. Turn right on C.R. 334 and go 3 miles to C.R. 307.
16. Turn right on C.R. 307 and go 1 mile to C.R. 307A.
17. Turn left on C.R. 307A and go 3.4 miles to Main Street in Trenton.
18. Turn right on Main Street, and go one-half of a mile to Trenton City Hall and end of the route.

▲ *Manatee Springs-Cedar Key loop*

This 71-mile loop takes you from Manatee Springs, one of the state's prettiest state parks, to Cedar Key, a far-from-civilization town that has survived more than a few natural and human-induced disasters.

The ride is designed for one day, but if you want to spend several hours exploring Cedar Key, you might choose to spend the night there. It's a good midpoint. It's 35.6 miles from Manatee Springs to Cedar Key and 36 miles for the return trip.

Manatee Springs is about six miles west of Chiefland in Levy County, just a short distance from the Suwannee River. All of the route is on flat land in Levy County. Cedar Key, on the Gulf of Mexico, is the southernmost point of the ride.

Chiefland is on U.S. Highway 19-98 and is easy to reach from almost any place in the state. You may leave your car for the day or overnight at the state park by paying a small fee.

During hot weather, Manatee Springs is a popular spot for bathers cooling off in the crystal clear water. The flow from Manatee Springs is 116.9 million gallons of water daily, and the water temperature is always 71 degrees. The water flows for about 1,200 feet from the spring's head to join the Suwannee River. The river reaches the Gulf 23 miles downstream.

Besides the swimming, visitors flock to Manatee Springs for boating, fishing, camping and diving. Bass, bream, catfish and speckled perch are abundant. There's a boat ramp nearby, and the spring run and the Suwannee are well-suited for canoeing.

For centuries, Indians sought the abundant fish and game in the springs area, and naturalist William Bartram

Town of Cedar Key

visited the spring in 1774 during his journey through Florida.

Cypress, gum, ash and maple trees abound in the swamp along the river. White-tailed deer, raccoons, opossums and red squirrels frequently are seen in the 2,075-acre park. There's a nature trail through a hammock where sinkholes are common, and a boardwalk along one side of the spring run provides a view into the river swamp.

The roads leading to Cedar Key are extremely quiet. Only on the last few miles into town is there likely to be any traffic, and even then it's seldom heavy.

After you get on CountyRoad 330, you'll see a sign directing you to turn left onto C.R. 347. Don't turn there. Instead continue for another eight-tenths of a mile to where the road curves left. That's where C.R. 330 runs into C.R. 347 and continues south. You'll encounter a fairly rough surface after about five miles on C.R. 347, but it's not bad. Let a little air out of your tires to reduce the pressure to about 50 if it does bother you.

Cedar Key is one of Florida's more historic towns. The road leading into town, State Road 24, has been built over a series of small keys through the marshland. You'll ride through this for a couple of miles before entering Cedar Key. State Road 24 is the only road into Cedar Key, so the town is quite isolated from the surrounding countryside. On the long stretch before reaching S.R. 24, you'll be in total wilderness with no signs of civilization for about 20 miles. Thickly wooded areas line the road, and there's little or no traffic.

Cedar Key has been battered by many hurricanes through the years, and it has survived a long series of misfortunes. The current population is only about 900, but late in the last century there were 5,000 residents here. Large stands of cedar trees in the area made Cedar Key the foremost producer of lead pencils in the United States. After Henry Plant built a railroad linking Tampa to the East Coast, the Cedar Key/Fernandina Beach rail line lost customers, and the town dwindled. When a 10-foot tidal surge from a hurricane in 1896 swept over

Cedar Key, it nearly finished the town.

Other disasters hit, including another bad hurricane in 1950, but the little town managed to stay in business and is now largely a fishing village. There are several good seafood restaurants, and there are adequate places to stay for the night. The famous Island Hotel, built in 1846 and in continuous operation ever since, has 10 rooms for rent and a dining room that serves good seafood dinners.

There's an interesting museum on the main business street, and the state operates another that's a short distance from S.R. 24. The state's museum is closed on Tuesday and Wednesday. Both museums provide interesting exhibits that depict the colorful history of Cedar Key and the surrounding area.

You can get a brochure at the private museum that details an excellent walking tour of the town. There are pictures and descriptions of 38 houses and buildings, most of them dating back to the 19th century. The tour can be accomplished in little more than an hour.

You'll take S.R. 24 out of town and continue on it for almost 10 miles before turning north on C.R. 345. This road is somewhat smoother than C.R. 347 that you took on your way to Cedar Key. After that you'll be on the same roads you pedaled over at the beginning of the ride until your return to the state park.

A swim in the cool waters of Manatee Springs will be a well-earned reward after pedaling more than 70 miles through the north Florida wilderness.

Because Cedar Key is the only town you'll visit on this route, be sure you have plenty of drinking water when you leave the state park. There's a little store a short distance from the park, and then nothing for more than 25 miles until you reach Cedar Key. On your return trip,

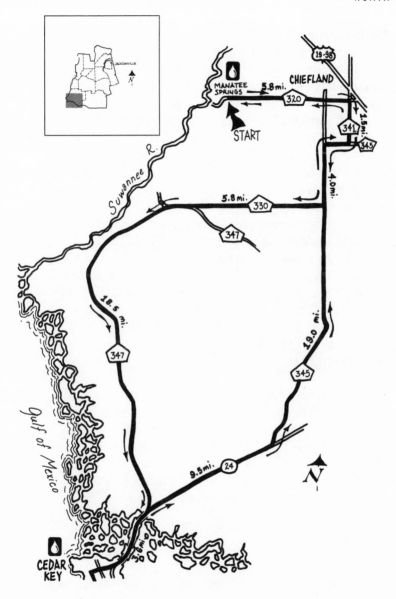

MANATEE SPRINGS

START

CHIEFLAND

19-98

5.8 mi.

320

1.5 mi.

341

345

4.0 mi.

Suwannee R.

5.8 mi.

330

347

18.5 mi.

347

19.0 mi.

345

Gulf of Mexico

9.5 mi.

24

N

3.8 mi.

CEDAR KEY

JACKSONVILLE

N

there's a small store on S.R. 24, and then only wilderness until your return to Manatee Springs.

This is a delightful trip at any time of the year, but plan to go between April and October if you want to fully savor a cooling swim in the springs. At other times of the year, the park is always a pretty spot, and Cedar Key is unchanged at any time of the year. It's a unique place to stop for either a short visit or a stay of several hours. No small town in the state has a more colorful history than this one.

Manatee Springs-Cedar Key loop

1. Go straight from main gate at Manatee Springs State Park for 5.8 miles on C.R. 320 to C.R. 341.
2. Turn right on C.R. 341 and go 1.5 miles to C.R. 345.
3. Turn right on C.R. 345 and go 4 miles to C.R. 330.
4. Turn right on C.R. 330 and go 5.8 miles to C.R. 347. DO NOT turn left at arrow pointing to C.R. 347.
5. Turn left at large curve where C.R. 347 joins C.R. 330 and go 18.5 miles to S.R. 24.
6. Turn right on S.R. 24 and go 3.6 miles to city park on 2nd Street in Cedar Key.
7. Begin return from city park. Go two-tenths of a mile to S.R. 24.
8. Turn right on S.R. 24 and go 9.5 miles to C.R. 345.
9. Turn left on C.R. 345 and go 19 miles to C.R. 341.
10. Turn left on C.R. 341 and go 1.5 miles to C.R. 320.
11. Turn left on C.R. 320 and go 5.8 miles to Manatee Springs State Park and end of route.

3. Central

▲ Bunnell-Old Dixie Highway loop

Take a ride down the Old Dixie Highway to see Florida as it appeared to the Seminole Indians and other tribes that were roaming the peninsula hundreds of years ago.

Once a main north-south thoroughfare for tourists and other travelers, the Old Dixie Highway is used mostly by locals. Tucked away in Flagler and Volusia counties, the road belongs to Florida's past and is relatively unknown even to the state's longtime residents.

This 57-mile loop starts and ends in Bunnell and is designed for a one-day ride. It is one of the most scenic and most interesting rides in Florida.

Don't be discouraged by the ride's start in Bunnell—it's not impressive. The county seat of Flagler County is a town with a population of about 2,000. One of the least populated counties in Florida, Flagler had only 3,367 residents in the 1950 census. This jumped to 10,913 by 1980, and that figure will have more than doubled in the 1990 census. Demographic specialists say Flagler is the fastest growing county in Florida, most of it because of the sprawling Palm Coast development along the Atlantic coast.

You should have no problem parking your car for the day in Bunnell. There usually is space in the area around the county courthouse building and the city hall building behind that. If you're riding on a weekend, most of those areas will be empty. During the week there are other areas in the business district for parking.

The turn onto Old Dixie Highway is about six miles south of Bunnell, off U.S. Highway 1. Traffic on this road is not heavy. It's a divided four-lane highway, so passing traffic will have plenty of room to get around you.

There's an immediate change of scenery after you turn onto Old Dixie Highway. It's heavily wooded country, and the trees form a canopy over most of the road. Though it's an old road, it has been well-maintained and is great for biking.

Within three miles, you'll see a sign on your left that is marked Volusia 2001 and Old Kings Highway. Turn here and go two miles to another sign pointing to the Bulow Plantation Ruins. It's a one-mile trip from here to the ruins over a sand road, but most of it is packed hard enough to ride a bike.

While this side trip is optional, a visit to the Bulow ruins is recommended. The ruins now are a state historic site and maintained by the Florida Department of Natural Resources. Open daily from 8 a.m. until 5 p.m., the site is in a beautiful natural setting. The plantation dates to the early 1800s when settlers started establishing plantations on Seminole Indian lands.

Maj. Charles Wilhelm Bulow acquired the 4,675 acres of land where the ruins are in 1821 and planted sugar cane, cotton and rice after slave labor had cleared more than 2,000 acres. Soon after getting the plantation established, Bulow died and left everything to his only son, John. The latter increased production, and the plantation prospered until the outbreak of the Second Seminole War. John James Audubon visited the plantation in 1831 and described Bulow as a rich planter at whose plantation he received hospitable treatment.

Though Bulow was friendly toward the Indians and even fired on state militia when they entered his property, he was taken prisoner by the Indians. The troops later withdrew to St. Augustine, and Bulow, realizing that the Indians were becoming more hostile, abandoned the plantation and followed the troops north. About Jan. 31, 1836, the Seminoles burned Bulowville and other plantations in the area, and Bulow, discouraged by this disastrous event, moved to Paris and died three months later at the age of 26.

All that's left now are the coquina ruins of the sugar mill, several wells, a spring house and the crumbling foundation of the mansion. The fields have been reclaimed by the forest, so the area appears much the same as it did when the Seminoles owned it.

The sugar mill ruins can be reached by a one-way loop drive or a scenic trail. There's a picnic area at the site, and scenic Bulow Creek, now a state canoe trail, is at the edge of the site.

After returning to the Old Dixie Highway, you'll ride only a half-mile before spotting a blue and white sign on your left that marks the Volusia County Scenic Trail. This is another side trip, but it's well worth the extra seven

BULOW SUGAR MILL
This was the largest sugar mill in Florida. It was operated by Charles Wilhelm Bulow and John Joachim Bulow from 1820 until it was burned by the Seminoles in 1836.
Sugar cane was planted in January and February and was ready for harvesting by mid-October. Field workers cut the cane and loaded it on wagons that brought it to the mill for processing.

miles you'll ride. The route crosses Bulow Creek after a short distance, then travels through wilderness country until a drawbridge that crosses the Halifax River, part of the Intracoastal Waterway.

From the drawbridge, it's only a short distance to State Road A1A and the Atlantic Ocean. On a hot day, this is a good place to stop for a swim. There's a good beach here, and it's never crowded. You'll cover the same road again as you return to Old Dixie Highway, but this scenery is worth a second look.

A little over a mile after you're back on Old Dixie Highway, you'll come to a little park with picnic tables and restrooms. It's the James Ormond Park, named for the man whose tomb is there. Ormond and his father migrated to Florida via the Bahamas in 1804. The younger Ormond was prominent in civil affairs and commanded a platoon during the Seminole War of 1836. The town of Ormond Beach was named for his family.

There will be four more miles on the Old Dixie Highway before turning onto Addison Drive. This road takes you back to U.S. Highway 1. There will be 10 more miles on this road, which is still four-laned, then about 17 more miles on country roads before you return to Bunnell.

Be sure to fill your water bottles before leaving Bunnell. There's water available at the Bulow Plantation Ruins and one convenience store on U.S. Highway 1, but that's it. For those wanting to crowd another day of riding into the weekend, there's another good loop not far away. That would be the ride from St. Augustine that goes along the Atlantic for more than 20 miles. It's also a one-day trip of about 55 miles. St. Augustine is 30 miles north of Bunnell.

Bunnell-Old Dixie Highway loop

1. Turn left on U.S. Highway 1 after leaving courthouse in Bunnell and go 5.7 miles to Old Dixie Highway.
2. Turn left on Old Dixie Highway and go 3.1 miles to Volusia 2001 (Old Kings Highway).
3. Turn left on Volusia 2001 and go 2 miles to sand road into Bulow Plantation Ruins.
4. Turn right on sand road and go 1 mile to ruins.
5. Return on the sand road and turn left on Volusia 2001.
6. Go 2 miles on Volusia 2001 to Old Dixie Highway.
7. Turn left on Old Dixie Highway and go one-half of a mile to Volusia County Scenic Route.
8. Turn left on Volusia County Scenic Route and go 3.4 miles to S.R. A1A.
9. Return on Volusia County Scenic Route for 3.4 miles and turn left onto Old Dixie Highway.
10. Go 5.3 miles on Old Dixie Highway to Addison Drive.
11. Turn right on Addison Drive and go 2.1 miles to U.S. Highway 1.
12. Turn right on U.S. Highway 1 and go 9.6 miles to C.R. 304.
13. Turn left on C.R. 304 and go 8 miles to S.R. 11.
14. Turn right on S.R. 11 and go 8.8 miles to parking lot near courthouse and end of route.

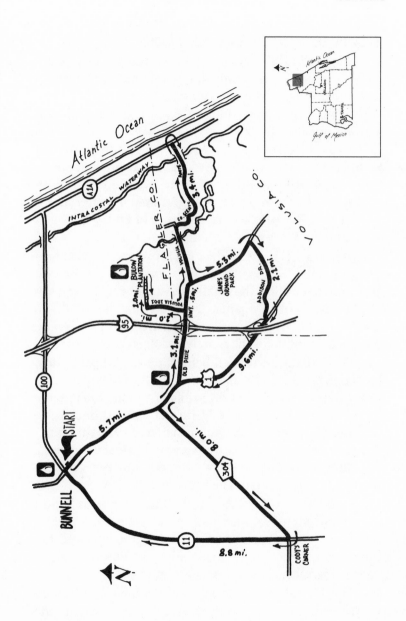

Atlantic Ocean

INTRA COSTAL WATERWAY

FLAGLER CO.

VOLUSIA CO.

A1A

3.4 mi.

BULOW PLANTATION

1.0 mi.

2.0 mi.

VOLUSIA HWY. 5681.

5.3 mi.

JAMES ORMOND PARK

2.1 mi.

ADDISON DR.

95

3.1 mi.

OLD DIXIE

1

9.6 mi.

100

START

5.7 mi.

BUNNELL

304

8.0 mi.

11

8.8 mi.

CODY'S CORNER

N

▲Dade Battlefield-Okahumpka loop

One of Florida's bloodiest battles occurred near Bushnell — the starting and finishing point for an 82-mile loop through Sumter and Lake counties.

In the state's early history there was no more disastrous event than the Indian ambush that killed 106 officers and men of the U.S. Army. The Dade Battlefield State Historic Site, on the outskirts of Bushnell about 50 miles west of Orlando, is a pretty, wooded park with picnic areas, a meeting building, a visitor center and a parking lot. But on the cold morning of Dec. 28, 1835, it was total wilderness.

Maj. Francis L. Dade, the man for whom Dade County was named, was leading relief units from Fort Brooke (Tampa) to reinforce the small garrison at Fort King, now Ocala, and protect against trouble from the Seminole Indians. There were 108 officers and men on this 100-mile march; two-thirds of the march had been completed.

The Indians, concealed behind pines and palmettos, had been observing the march for five days. They opened fire about 8 a.m. The first rifle volley from the 180 Indians killed or wounded half of Dade's command, including the major. The second onslaught lasted until about 2 p.m., when all the firing by the troops ceased. Most were dead, but three wounded soldiers escaped, and two of them made it to Fort Brooke. The third man died en route.

Seven weeks passed before another Army expedition found and identified the bodies and gave them proper burial with military rites. Six years later, in 1842, the bodies were moved to the National Cemetery in St. Augustine where the silent command now rests.

This historic site is open Thursday through Monday from 8 a.m. to sunset. There is an interpretive trail in the park, and exhibits and artifacts in the visitor center are worth seeing.

There's a small fee for parking your car there for the day, but don't plan to return after sunset since the park is closed.

Most of this loop is in Sumter County; more than 20 miles are in Lake County. The route is almost entirely on quiet roads through farming country and what remains of once-prosperous citrus groves. Nearly all citrus was destroyed in the freezes of 1983 and 1985. A few optimistic grove owners replanted, but another freeze in December 1989 killed much of that planting.

Despite the grim sight of dead citrus trees and cleared land where the trees used to be, this is a pretty ride. A good portion of it is in wooded areas on roads almost devoid of traffic.

After leaving the battlefield site, there will be about a mile through Bushnell, which is the county seat of Sumter County. After that you're quickly onto rural roads. The first of these is County Road 747. It's marked with a small sign, but a Church of God campground sign on the corner is more evident. Triton Technologies Inc. will be on your left at this turn.

You have more than two miles down a narrow road canopied with large oak trees before you get to C.R. 478, which will take you into the town of Webster. If you're making this ride on Monday, visit the Farmers' Market there. It's only a few blocks off your route, and it's one of the largest of its kind in Florida. Besides all the fresh produce for sale, there are hundreds of booths selling the usual flea market merchandise.

It's about six miles from Webster to the town of Center Hill. Though the population is more than 700, the business district here is almost a ghost town. There are two blocks of boarded-up store fronts and only a few small businesses still functioning.

Three miles out of Center Hill, watch closely for the turn onto C.R. 278. There's a sign there for the Tuscanooga Baptist Church. This is another pretty road through unpopulated country with thick woods on both sides.

You'll return to civilization in the town of Mascotte on State Road 50. This is a busy highway, but it slows through the town, and you'll have only seven-tenths of a mile before you turn onto C.R. 50. This is another road that you'll have to watch for closely. It will be on your left just before the Circle K convenience store on your right.

The short stretch through Mascotte will be the only real traffic you'll encounter on the route.

From Mascotte you'll soon be on C.R. 33, and the next turn will be on the Austin-Merritt Road. It will be the first road after Mascotte on your left. This will take you back to the edge of Center Hill, and from here you'll pick up C.R. 48 and pedal another nine miles to the crossroads community of Okahumpka.

After you pass Okahumpa and you're pedaling on C.R. 471, look carefully for C.R. 567 — it's easy to miss. A sign on the right indicates that it is C.R. 476 West, but you'll turn left here. You have 2.5 miles on this country road that rarely has any traffic other than bicycles. It's a pretty stretch leading to C.R. 48. From here you have just a few more miles back to Bushnell and the Dade Battlefield parking lot.

Sumter County is one of the very few Central Florida counties that didn't experience spectacular growth during the '70s and '80s. It's strictly rural and relies heavily on truck crops. It has changed little over the years, and the prospects of any major changes in the future are slight. Despite hills, it's a great county for cycling. The quiet roads and a visit to the historic site combine for an interesting loop.

If 82 miles seem excessive for a single day, there's an alternate route that cuts 22 miles. This can be done by eliminating the 22-mile leg of the ride that goes to Mascotte. When you get into Center Hill from C.R. 478 and turn right on C.R. 48, turn left on the east side of the town at the junction of C.R. 469 and C.R. 48. By turning left you stay on C.R. 48 to Okahumpka. After Okahumpka the route will be the same.

Dade Battlefield-Okahumpka loop

1. Exit the Dade Battlefield and go three-tenths of a mile on Battlefield Drive to C.R. 476.
2. Turn right on C.R. 476 and go one-half of a mile to traffic light at U. S. Highway 301. C.R. 476 also becomes C.R. 48 after crossing U.S. Highway 301.
3. Continue on C.R. 476-48 for three-tenths of a mile to C.R. 48.
4. Turn right on C.R. 48 and go 2.4 miles to C.R. 747.
5. Turn right on C.R. 747 and go 2.5 miles to C.R. 478.
6. Turn left on C.R. 478 and go 1.3 miles to C.R. 471 in town of Webster.
7. Turn right on C.R. 471 and go four-tenths of a mile to C.R. 478.
8. Turn left on C.R. 478 and go 6.2 miles to C.R. 48 in town of Center Hill.
9. Turn right on C.R. 48 and go three-tenths of a mile to C.R. 469.
10. Go straight ahead on C.R. 469 and go 2.8 miles to C.R. 728.
11. Turn left on C.R. 728 and go 5.6 miles to S.R. 50 in town of Mascotte.

12. Turn left on S.R. 50 and go seven-tenths of a mile to C.R. 50. Circle K store is on the right at turn.

13. Turn left on C.R. 50 and go seven-tenths of a mile to C.R. 33.

14. Turn left on C.R. 33 and go 6.5 miles to Austin-Merritt Road. Sign for Bridge Road is on right.

15. Turn left on Austin-Merritt Road and go 6.2 miles to C.R. 48 near Center Hill.

16. Turn right on C.R. 48 and go 8.4 miles to C.R. 33 and C.R. 48.

17. Turn left on C.R. 33 and 48 and go one-half of a mile to C.R. 470 in town of Okahumpka.

18. Turn left on C.R. 470 and go 10.6 miles to U.S. Highway 301.

19. Turn left on U.S. Highway 301 and go two-tenths of a mile to C.R. 471.

20. Turn left on C.R. 471 and go 6.3 miles to C.R. 567. C.R. 476 is on the right.

21. Turn left on C.R. 567 and go 2.5 miles to C.R. 48.

22. Turn right on C.R. 48 and go 5.2 miles to C.R. 476 in town of Bushnell.

23. Turn left on C.R. 476 and go nine-tenths of a mile to Battlefield Drive.

24. Turn left on Battlefield Drive and go three-tenths of a mile back to starting point at Dade Battlefield.

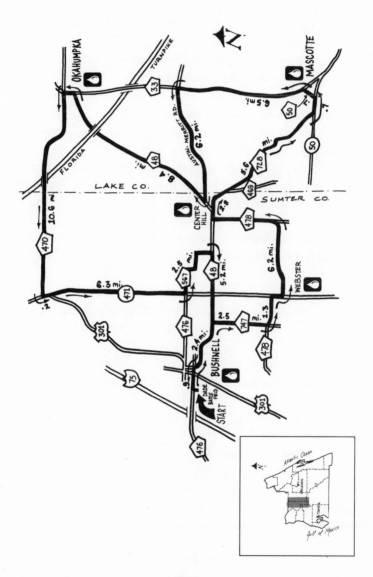

▲ DeLand-Umatilla loop

Some of Central Florida's finest scenery is included in this loop. You'll begin your ride in DeLand, stop in Umatilla overnight, then travel through the towns of Eustis, Tavares and Mount Dora before crossing the St. Johns River and returning to DeLand.

This one is a century — 49 miles from DeLand to Umatilla and 51 miles on the second day.

If you're looking for alternatives to stopping at a motel in Umatilla, there are two full-facility campgrounds — both managed by the National Forest Service — before you reach that town. The Lake Dorr Recreation Area, only a few miles before Umatilla, has a nice lake for swimming. Several miles before that is the Alexander Springs Recreation Area, which has a natural spring-fed swimming area. Both are in the Ocala National Forest.

Staying at either campground will mean fewer miles on the first day's ride and more miles on the second — not enough, however, to make the longer day a tough ride.

Begin your ride in DeLand, the home of Stetson University. The town, with a population of about 20,000, is known for its many well-kept old homes and shaded streets. Park your car at the Department of Transportation building on Woodland Boulevard.

Head north on Woodland Boulevard, DeLand's main business street, until you reach the Stetson University campus. Turn west onto Minnesota Avenue and ride through an attractive residential district. After you turn onto Grand Avenue, the four-mile mark on the route, you'll be treated to more than six miles of outstanding suburban scenery. The route goes through heavily wooded sections with homes on large, well-landscaped lots. The trees form a canopy over the road for much of this stretch, which goes through the community of Glenwood before reaching the historic town of DeLeon Springs.

The area around DeLeon Springs first was settled in 1804. Cotton, corn and sugar cane were raised. A gristmill, which used the spring for power, was added in 1823. John James Audubon visited the spring in 1832.

The name DeLeon Springs first appeared in the late 1800s, when the railroad arrived and with it the promotion of the area as a winter resort. An advertisement in 1889 claimed the spring was a Fountain of Youth. Over the years, a myth identifying the springs as Juan Ponce de Leon's Fountain of Youth has grown.

The site now is the DeLeon Springs State Recreation Area. Swimming, picnicking, canoeing and fishing are offered, and facilities include a good restaurant and snack bar. The sugar mill still stands.

From the park the route continues on a quiet road that originally was U.S. Highway 17. After a little more than seven miles, you'll turn onto Emporia Road, another quiet byway that goes through the community of Emporia. This wooded country is real back roads Florida.

About halfway through the first day of the loop, the route enters State Road 40. There's some traffic here, but it's not heavy. You'll cross the St. Johns River over the new Astor drawbridge, and there are several places offering good catfish and seafood meals.

Just before leaving S.R. 40 and heading south to County Road 445 you'll enter the Ocala National Forest, one of Florida's largest. After six miles on this road, lined on both sides with thick woods, you'll have time for a break at the Alexander Springs Recreation Area. The huge spring pours out 80 million gallons of water each day.

From here the route continues for about 10 more miles to the town of Altoona. You're on S.R. 19 now, and you'll ride three more miles to Umatilla.

Umatilla is a town of about 2,000. It has several good eating spots, but there is only one motel. It's on your left on S.R. 19 in the business section. Though S.R. 19 is busy south of Altoona, there's a shoulder lane for bikes to Umatilla, then a divided four-lane highway until you leave S.R. 19 in downtown Eustis.

Stay alert to spot the Lakeshore Drive sign when leaving S.R. 19. It will be on your right. If you turn left, you'll be on Citrus Avenue. This is in the business section of Eustis. Lake Eustis will be on your right, and you will see Waterman Memorial Hospital on your left about two blocks before making your turn.

One of the more scenic portions of the trip is the three-mile stretch on Lakeshore Drive from Eustis to U.S. Highway 441. With the big lake on your right and beautiful homes on well-shaded lots on your left, it's an enjoyable ride.

The only really busy road of the entire trip is less than a half-mile sprint on U.S. Highway 441. Use extreme caution. It's heavy traffic at fairly high speed on a divided four-lane road. Head for the left-hand lane as soon as you turn onto U.S. Highway 441 and stay there until the second traffic light, where you turn left onto C.R. 452 (St. Clair-Abrams Street). You're in the town of Tavares now. Continue on St. Clair-Abrams Street until you turn left onto Main Street in downtown Tavares.

Now you can enjoy another scenic ride along Lake Dora for nearly five miles to the picturesque town of Mount Dora. The lake is on one side and many large homes are on the other. The route misses the business section, but you'll pedal through some nice residential areas to C.R. 44B (Donnelly Street).

After leaving Mount Dora, the rest of the route will be strictly rural until your return to DeLand. Some of this area was hard hit by the freezes of 1983 and 1985 that wiped out thousands of acres of citrus trees. Most of it, though, is pasture land and woods. The traffic is light. You'll pass through only one town after leaving Mount Dora — Paisley, a town of a few hundred citizens.

There will be more than 15 miles on S.R. 42 before you turn onto S.R. 44. You're immediately into heavier traffic, though it's not bad. You'll cross the St. Johns River at the Whitehair Bridge. The road leads to DeLand, and you'll stay on it into downtown DeLand. Turn the first block past Woodland Boulevard, the street where you started your ride on the first day. It's a short ride back to the parking lot at the Department of Transportation building.

This route features a great variety of scenery. In addition to a good look at the back roads of the area, you'll pass through some of the state's prettiest towns. You will cross the St. Johns River twice, ride through several miles of a national forest and pass two National Forest Service campgrounds and one state recreation area. The two rides along beautiful lakes in Eustis and between Tavares and Mount Dora, the suburban ride after leaving DeLand and a pass through the little towns of DeLeon Springs, Astor, Altoona and Umatilla make this one of the best two-day rides in Florida.

DeLand-Umatilla loop

1. Turn right on Woodland Boulevard out of the Department of Transportation building parking lot

and go 1.4 miles to Minnesota Avenue.

2. Turn left on Minnesota Avenue and go 2.6 miles to Grand Avenue. Grand Avenue goes left here for a short distance, then turns right.

3. Go 6.5 miles on Grand Avenue to Baxter Street.

4. Turn left on Baxter Street and go one-tenth of a mile to Cortez Street.

5. Turn right on Cortez Street and go six-tenths of a mile to Park .

6. Turn right on Park and go two-tenths of a mile to Ponce de Leon Boulevard.

7. Turn left on Ponce de Leon Boulevard and go one-tenth of a mile to DeLeon Springs Recreation Area.

8. Turn right at DeLeon Springs Recreation Area and go 7.6 miles on C.R. 3 to Emporia Road.

9. Turn left on Emporia Road and go 5.2 miles to S.R. 40.

10. Turn right on S.R. 40 and go 4 miles to C.R. 445A.

11. Turn left on C.R. 445A and go one-half of a mile to the junction of C.R. 415A and C.R. 445.

12. Turn left on C.R. 445 and go 11.1 miles to S.R. 19.

13. Turn left on S.R. 19 and go 13.3 miles through towns of Altoona and Umatilla to Lakeshore Drive in town of Eustis.

14. Turn right on Lakeshore Drive and go 3.3 miles to U.S. Highway 441.

15. Turn right on U.S. Highway 441 and go four-tenths of a mile to C.R. 452 (St. Clair-Abrams) in town of Tavares.

16. Turn left on C.R. 452 and go 1 mile to Main Street in Tavares.

17. Turn left on Main Street, which becomes Lake Dora Drive, then Lakeshore Drive, and go 4.8 miles to 11th Avenue in town of Mount Dora. Lakeshore becomes 11th Avenue after crossing railroad tracks and Old

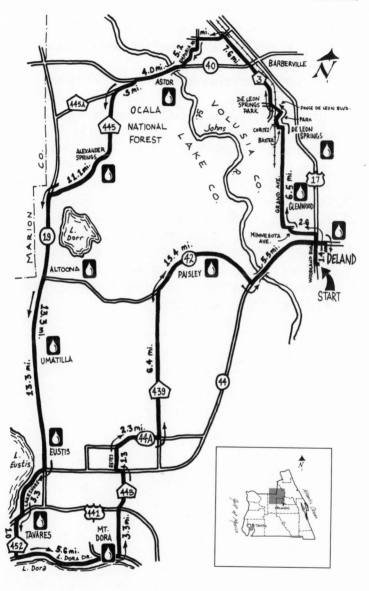

U.S. Highway 441 and passing "Y" intersection.

18. Go eight-tenths of a mile on 11th Avenue to Donnelly Street (C.R. 44B).

19. Turn left on Donnelly Street and go 3.3 miles to S.R. 44.

20. Turn left on S.R. 44 and go three-tenths of a mile to Estes Road.

21. Turn right on Estes Road and go 1.3 miles to S.R. 44A.

22. Turn right on S.R. 44A and go 2.3 miles to C.R. 439.

23. Turn left on C.R. 439 and go 6.4 miles to S.R. 42.

24. Turn right on S.R. 42 and go 15.4 miles to S.R. 44.

25. Turn left on S.R. 44, cross St. Johns River and go 5.5 miles to Alabama Street in town of DeLand.

26. Turn right on Alabama Street and go nine-tenths of a mile to Department of Transportation building parking lot and end of ride.

▲ Lake Wales-Haines City loop

Central Florida's Polk County produces more citrus than the entire state of California. It's an excellent place to pedal between the orange and grapefruit trees and alongside the area's many pretty lakes.

Citrus is just about everywhere in Polk County. If it's not being grown, it's being packed in processing plants for shipment around the United States.

Lake Wales, a town of about 9,000, is a good place to start and finish this 100-mile trip. The ride can be split for a two-day trip with 35 miles on the first day and 65 miles on the second. Haines City is the suggested overnight stopping point.

If you choose to take two days to enjoy this route, you'll have time to see the sights around Lake Wales. Bok Tower Gardens is just outside town, and the Black Hills Passion Play is staged during Lent each year. A fascinating town museum in an old train depot is worth a visit, and Spook Hill is a popular spot where a car seems to roll mysteriously uphill backwards when you put it in neutral and take your foot off the brake.

You can begin your trip anywhere in Lake Wales, but the Sun Bank parking lot downtown is recommended. It's a safe place to leave your car for the weekend and a good central location if you're planning to visit the attractions.

It's only about two miles to get out of town into the rural areas and citrus groves. This county escaped much of the damage during the disastrous 1983 and 1985 freezes, so most of the trees are large and loaded with fruit. In late March and early April the delightful smell of orange blossoms fills the air.

Lakes, both large and small, are scattered along the

179

Bok Tower

route, and much of the terrain is gently rolling. Traffic is light on nearly all the roads you'll travel.

Take a break in Dundee, the first town you'll enter after leaving Lake Wales. This is close to the 20-mile mark on the first day. From here the route turns north to the town of Lake Hamilton.

There are many twists and turns on this route, so pay close attention to your map and directions. After you leave Dundee, the next turn you'll make will be onto Bryant Street. There's no sign marking the street; turn left on the first paved road you reach in Lake Hamilton.

Between Lake Hamilton and Haines City there's some scenic country that includes nice residential sections around the lakes and many oak and cypress trees.

In Haines City there are some older motels in the downtown section and a newer motel on U.S. Highway 27. This is only a short distance from downtown, but getting there involves riding a couple of miles on U.S. Highway 27, a busy four-lane divided highway. There are plenty of restaurants in town.

After riding through Davenport the second day, the route soon reaches Old Kissimmee Road, one of the state's few remaining brick highways. It was a busy road back in the 1920s, but it's almost devoid of traffic now, and it's rough. It passes through thick woods. You'll feel as if you're miles from civilization.

There's a short stretch on U.S. Highway 17-92 before you reach another historic road, the Old Tampa Highway. It's a narrow three-mile strip that ends at Poinciana, a large residential development in Osceola County.

From Poinciana, it is almost 20 miles through mostly undeveloped country. It's great biking here—almost no traffic, good roads and flat terrain.

As you near the last 20 miles of your trip, you re-enter

citrus country. Huge groves line both sides of the road for miles. You'll make many turns in this part of the ride, but whenever you turn you'll find more citrus trees.

Toward the end of the ride you'll pass a side road that leads into the grounds where the Passion Play is staged each year.

As you re-enter Lake Wales you'll pass some nice residential areas and ride around the lake the town is named for before you return to the parking lot at the ride's end.

For an experienced rider determined to cover as many miles as possible in a day, this ride can be handled without an overnight stop. For those who want to enjoy the scenery, smell the orange blossoms and appreciate one of the state's most delightful areas, two days is recommended.

Lake Wales-Haines City loop

1. Turn left out of Sun Bank parking lot on Central Avenue and go 1.3 miles to S.R. 60.
2. Turn right on S.R. 60 and go four-tenths of a mile to Old Bartow Road.
3. Turn right on Old Bartow Road and go 4.5 miles to C.R. 653. Old Bartow Road goes left and C.R. 653 is straight ahead.
4. Continue on C.R. 653 for 2.7 miles to C.R. 540A.
5. Turn right on C.R. 540A and go one-half of a mile to where road becomes Thompson Nursery Road.
6. Continue on Thompson Nursery Road for 2.9 miles, when road becomes C.R. 17A after crossing U.S. Highway 27.
7. Continue on C.R. 17A for 1.8 miles to U.S. Highway 27A.
8. Turn left on U.S. Highway 27A and go 5.4 miles to

flashing light in town of Dundee.

9. Turn right at flashing light and go 1.7 miles to Bryant Street which is not marked.

10. Turn left on Bryant Street in town of Lake Hamilton and go two-tenths of a mile to Omaha Street.

11. Turn left on Omaha and go one-tenth of a mile to Sample Street.

12. Turn right on Sample Street and go three-tenths of a mile to 6th Street.

13. Turn left on 6th Street and go one-tenth of a mile to Main Street.

14. Turn right on Main Street and go one-half of a mile to U.S. Highway 27, where Main Street becomes Crump Road.

15. Continue on Crump Road for 2.2 miles to Country Club Road.

16. Turn right on Country Club Road and go 1.7 miles to West Lake Hamilton Drive.

17. Turn right on West Lake Hamilton Drive and go 2.9 miles to C.R. 544.

18. After stopping in Haines City, turn right on C.R. 544 and go 3.5 miles to 30th Street.

19. Turn left on 30th Street and go 1.5 miles to Hinson Street.

20. Turn right on Hinson Street, and go 1 mile to Power Line Road.

21. Turn left on Power Line Road and go 3.4 miles to South Boulevard in town of Davenport.

22. Turn left on South Boulevard and go six-tenths of a mile to Suwannee Street.

23. Turn right on Suwannee Street and go four-tenths of a mile to Bay Street.

24. Turn left on Bay Street and go two-tenths of a mile to C.R. 547.

25. Turn right on C.R. 547 and go 6.7 miles to C.R. 54.

26. Turn right on C.R. 54 and go two-tenths of a mile to Old Kissimmee Road (brick).
27. Turn left on Old Kissimmee Road and go 1.8 miles to Osceola-Polk county line.
28. Turn right on Osceola-Polk Line Road and go one-tenth of a mile to U.S. Highway 17-92.
29. Turn left on U.S. Highway 17-92 and go eight-tenths of a mile to Old Tampa Highway.
30. Turn left on Old Tampa Highway and go 3 miles to Poinciana Boulevard.
31. Turn right on Poinciana Boulevard and go 8.4 miles to Pleasant Hill Road.
32. Turn right on Pleasant Hill Road and go six-tenths of a mile to Cypress Parkway.
33. Turn right on Cypress Parkway and go 1.7 miles to Marigold Avenue.
34. Turn left on Marigold Avenue and go 9.6 miles to C.R. 542.
35. Turn right on C.R. 542 and go 1.9 miles to Watkins Road.
36. Turn left on Watkins Road and go 2.2 miles to Canal Road.
37. Turn right on Canal Road and go 2.1 miles to Timberlane Road.
38. Turn left on Timberlane Road and go 2.9 miles to C.R. 17A.
39. Turn left on C.R. 17A and go 3.9 miles to C.R. 17B.
40. Turn left on C.R. 17B and go nine-tenths of a mile to Sunset Drive.
41. Turn left on Sunset Drive and go one-half of a mile to Evergreen Drive.
42. Turn right on Evergreen Drive and go one-half of a mile to S.R. 60, where Evergreen Drive becomes Lewis Griffin Road.

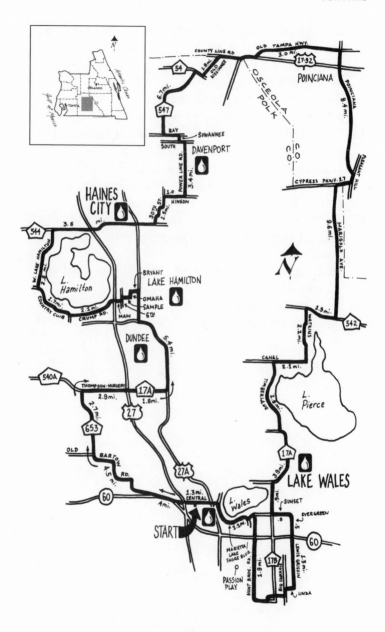

43. Continue on Lewis Griffin Road 1.3 miles to Linda Street.
44. Turn right on Linda Street and go two-tenths of a mile to Big Sinkhole Road.
45. Turn left on Big Sinkhole Road and go two-tenths of a mile to Garfield Nursery Road.
46. Turn right on Garfield Nursery Road and go one-half of a mile to Hunt Brothers Road, also C.R. 17B.
47. Turn right on Hunt Brothers Road-C.R. 17B and go 1.9 miles to Sunset Drive. Hunt Brothers Road becomes 11th Street after crossing S.R. 60.
48. Turn left on Sunset Drive and go three-tenths of a mile to Marietta Street, which becomes Lake Shore Boulevard.
49. Turn right on Marietta-Lake Shore Boulevard and 1.1 miles to Central Avenue.
50. Turn left on Central Avenue and go one-half of a mile to parking lot and end of route.

▲ *Mount Dora-Clermont loop*

This loop from Mount Dora to Clermont and back will give riders a chance to pedal 100 miles in two days and explore some of Florida's more interesting countryside.

More experienced cyclists might prefer to do this route in one day, but for families and less stout-hearted pedalers, this is an ideal weekend trip. It's 65 miles to Clermont and 35 miles on the return trip to Mount Dora.

This route offers a variety of scenery and enough hills to make it challenging. You'll encounter hills after leaving Astatula on County Road 455. And from the top of these hills, you'll be treated to wonderful views of the countryside that is dotted with lakes. This part of the ride is about three miles.

Howey-in-the Hills, one of Florida's prettiest small towns, is worth a stop. There's a convenience store there, and you may want to walk around the town. It's a neat and tidy place and very quiet. Big oak trees line the route on the way out of town.

On a six-mile stretch of C.R. 2 outside Howey, there's a rare sight of quite a few old citrus trees, survivors of the killer freezes of 1983 and 1985. Those freezes, the worst of the 20th century, devastated this area. Acres of trees have been planted next to the old trees that survived. It's a scenic ride on a narrow road that is almost devoid of traffic.

On C.R. 48, you'll cross U.S. Highway 27 — this is a busy highway — be careful.

County Road 33 goes through a long stretch of agricultural land that includes some replanted citrus and pasture.

Once in the small town of Mascotte, be careful crossing State Road 50 — it's a busy two-lane highway with heavy truck traffic.

There's a scenic five-mile ride on Erie Lake Road as you near the end of the first day's tour. Most of this stretch is heavily wooded, and you'll enjoy the sight of pretty Erie Lake on your left just before reaching C.R. 33.

When you reach C.R. 561, you can enjoy panoramic views of lakes and hills in all directions.

Clermont is the stopping point for the first day. There are about 25 restaurants, including most of the fast-food chains, and some locally owned places that offer good meals at reasonable prices. Several of these restaurants also are open for breakfast. There also are plenty of motels in town, though most of them are on U.S Highway 27, at the east side of Clermont.

The return trip to Mount Dora is much shorter, but it also offers some good scenery. Scenic Clermont is one of Florida's hilliest towns. The route goes through pleasant residential sections, then skirts Lake Minneola before entering the town of Minneola. If you're making this trip during hot weather, there's a nice beach on Lake Minneola that's on the route. Park your bike under a tree and dive in.

Some real climbing awaits you early on the second day as you approach the town of Montverde. There is a formidable series of hills before and after you leave the town. On C.R. 455 north of Montverde, there's a point where you'll want to stop and admire the view. You can see for miles, and Lake Apopka, one of Florida's largest, is in the distance.

From here you're ready for a trip up Sugarloaf Mountain. This is quite a climb by Florida standards, but it can be handled with any 10-speed bike. From here there are a few more hills to negotiate before reaching level ground on C.R. 561.

The last few miles of this day's ride will repeat part of the first day's ride.

A public parking lot in Mount Dora, at the corner of Fourth Avenue and Baker Street, is suggested as a starting point. It's a safe place to leave your car overnight and also is easily accessible to the Mount Dora business district. With that short second day, you'll have time to see the antiques shops and other sights around this town. Mount Dora, on the shores of Lake Dora, is a haven for retirees, who make up about 60 percent of the town's population.

All of this ride is in Lake County, and the towns at both ends are lovely. Mount Dora, except for the palm trees and Spanish moss, almost could pass for a town in New England. Clermont bills itself as "The Gem of the Hills," and it's an apt description. Though thousands of acres of citrus trees surrounding the town were destroyed in the 1983 and 1985 freezes, Clermont remains one of Florida's prettiest towns, and no place in the state has steeper hills.

The Great Green Swamp lies south of Mascotte. It's one of the state's most important ecological areas. It supplies much of Florida's drinking water and is the source of five major rivers, including the Withlacoochee, Hillsborough, Peace, Kissimmee and Oklawaha. Unlike most swamps, this one is more than 100 feet above sea level.

Mount Dora-Clermont loop:
1. Turn left out of parking lot onto Baker Street and go to Fourth Avenue.
2. Turn left on Fourth Avenue and go one block to Tremain Street.

3. Turn right on Tremain Street and go four-tenths of a mile to Gilbert Park and Liberty Avenue.

4. Turn left on Liberty Avenue and go one-tenth of a mile to Grandview Street.

5. Turn right on Grandview Street and go two-tenths of a mile to Johns Avenue.

6. Turn left on Johns Avenue and go two-tenths of a mile to Clayton Street.

7. Turn right on Clayton Street and go eight-tenths of a mile to Beauclair Drive.

8. Turn right on Beauclair Drive and go three-tenths of a mile to Dora Drive.

9. Turn left on Dora Drive and go 2.3 miles to Sadler Road (C.R. 448).

10. Turn right on C.R. 448 and go 1.3 miles to C.R. 448A. Beware of blind corner on right.

11. Turn left on C.R. 448A and go 1.5 miles to C.R. 48.

12. Turn right on C.R. 48 and go 4.4 miles to C.R. 561 (Monroe Street in town of Astatula).

13. Turn left on C.R. 561 and go 3 miles to C.R. 455.

14. Turn right on C.R. 455 and go 2.9 miles to State Road 19.

15. Turn right on S.R. 19 and go 2.5 miles to Florida Avenue in town of Howey-in-the-Hills.

16. Turn left on Florida Avenue and go one-half of a mile to West Central Avenue (C.R. 2).

17. Turn left on C.R. 2 and go 6 miles to C.R. 48.

18. Turn left on C.R. 48 and go 3.6 miles to C.R. 33.

19. Turn left on C.R. 33 and go 11.2 miles to C.R. 50.

20. Turn right on C.R. 50 and go nine-tenths of a mile to S.R. 50 in town of Mascotte. S.R. 50 is Massachusetts Street in Mascotte. Cross S.R. 50 and route becomes South Sunset, then Empire-Mascotte Road.

21. Go 3.3 miles on Sunset and Empire-Mascotte Road to Empire Church Road.

22. Turn right on Empire Church Road and go 1.2 miles to Bay Lake Road (C.R. 565).

23. Turn left on Bay Lake Road and go 3.8 miles to Erie Lake Road.

24. Turn left on Erie Lake Road and go 5.1 miles to S.R. 33.

25. Turn left on S.R. 33 and go 2.7 miles to C.R. 565B.

26. Turn right on C.R. 565B and go 3.7 miles to C.R. 561.

27. Turn left on C.R. 561 and go 4 miles to 12th Street in town of Clermont.

28. Turn left on 12th Street and go four-tenths of a mile to S.R. 50.

29. Starting on second day from S.R. 50 and 12th Street, cross S.R. 50 and go three-tenths of a mile to Minneola Avenue.

30. Turn right on Minneola Avenue and go four-tenths of a mile to 8th Street.

31. Turn left on 8th Street and go one-tenth of a mile to Lake Minneola Drive.

32. Turn right on Lake Minneola Drive (C.R. 561); go 1.7 miles to Washington Street in town of Minneola.

33. Turn right on Washington Street and go 4.8 miles to C.R. 455. Washington becomes Old 50 after leaving Minneola.

34. Turn left on C.R. 455 and go one-tenth of a mile to where C.R. 455 makes sharp turn to left and crosses over Florida Turnpike.

35. Turn left on C.R. 455 and go 10.6 miles to C.R. 561.

36. Turn right on C.R. 561 and go 7.2 miles to C.R. 448.

37. Turn right on C.R. 448 and go 4.8 miles to Lake Jem Road.

38. Turn left on Lake Jem Road and go one-tenth of a mile to East Lake Jem Road.

39. Turn right on East Lake Jem Road and go four-tenths of a mile to C.R. 448.
40. Turn left on C.R. 448 and go 1 mile to Dora Drive.
41. Turn left on Dora Drive and go 2.3 miles to Beauclair Street.
42. Turn right on Beauclair Street and go three-tenths of a mile to Clayton Street.
43. Turn left on Clayton Street and go eight-tenths of a mile to Johns Avenue.
44. Turn left on Johns Avenue and go two-tenths of a mile to Grandview Street.
45. Turn right on Grandview Street and go two-tenths of a mile to Liberty Avenue.
46. Turn left on Liberty Avenue and go one-tenth of a mile to Gilbert Park and Tremain Street.
47. Turn right on Tremain Street and go four-tenths of a mile to Fourth Avenue.
48. Turn left on Fourth Avenue and go one block to Baker Street.
49. Turn right on Baker Street and back to starting point in parking lot.

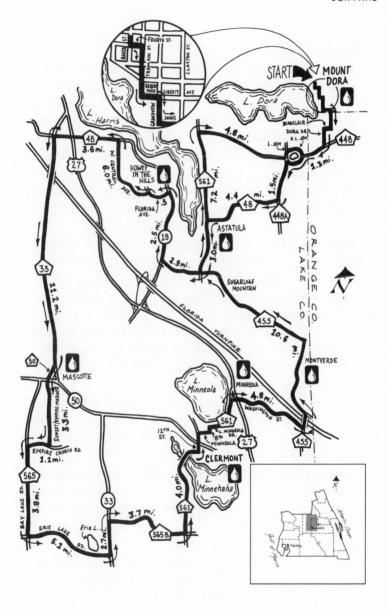

▲ Sugarloaf Mountain loop

Hills are not common in Florida, and mountains are non-existent. But in Lake County, northwest of Orlando, there's a route that has many fairly steep and challenging hills, and one hill that has been labeled a mountain. Sugarloaf Mountain is a good place to practice climbing.

The 64-mile route is entirely in Lake County except for a few-yard excursion into Orange County. There's plenty of good scenery and many twists and turns before you return to the starting point in downtown Mount Dora.

You won't have long to wait for the hills — Mount Dora is a hilly town. There also is no waiting for scenery. Less than two miles from the starting point, you'll be pedaling on Lakeshore Drive, a scenic five-mile ride along Lake Dora's edge. That portion of the ride ends when you arrive in Tavares. Be careful crossing the old railroad tracks when you enter Tavares' business district. The tracks form an oblique angle, and many bikers have had some nasty spills at the spot.

You may have trouble spotting the sign for Lake Avenue after going through downtown Tavares. It's on your left and somewhat faded. Look for a small grocery store — you'll turn left there.

Within a short distance, there will be several turns as you ride through a mobile home park before reaching State Road 19. It's a busy road at this point, so be careful for the few yards you're on it. Three turns later, and you're finally in hilly, rural country.

Young orange groves, planted after the disastrous freezes of 1983 and 1985, march up and down the hills, and Little Lake Harris is on your right.

There's a stretch of almost seven miles on County

Road 561 that takes you through the town of Astatula, a good place to refuel with cold drinks and snacks.

When you turn onto C.R. 455, get ready for more hill climbing. There are some good-sized ones here that will give your gears a workout, including your first ride on to Sugarloaf Mountain.

After a particularly long grind up Sugarloaf, you'll see Lake Apopka, one of Florida's largest lakes, in the distance. The lake used to be beautiful, famed for bass fishing, but now it's totally polluted — the bass left years ago.

The route goes through the small towns of Ferndale and Montverde, where there is a convenience store. You'll cross over Florida's Turnpike, then ride a few miles on Old Highway 50 to the outskirts of Minneola.

Just before arriving in Minneola, make a sharp turn onto the road entering Old Highway 50 on your right. You'll be on Grassy Lake Road.

Grassy Lake Road makes several turns, but it's the only hard-surfaced road around; you can't get lost. At one point the signs on the left-hand side of the road are marked Rockwell; nevertheless, it's still Grassy Lake Road.

There may be some confusion on this road later. Grassy Lake Road continues straight ahead, but a sign on a road turning to the right also is marked Grassy Lake Road. Turn right and continue until you reach C.R. 561A.

There's little more than a mile until you're on Sugarloaf Mountain Road.

While Sugarloaf has been touted as one of the really tough hills for biking in Florida, it's not that difficult. Slip into your lowest gear in the early stages, and you should have no problem making it. The climb is fairly easy if you have more than 10 gears. Before the big hill there are several other nearby climbs that aren't as long or as steep.

After Sugarloaf your hill climbing for the day is finished. You will return to the flatlands back to Mount Dora.

From the hilltops on Grassy Lake Road there are some outstanding views of the surrounding country — the lakes and the hills that are such an important part of this county. There are good photo opportunities on clear days.

There's no problem leaving your car at the public parking lot at the corner of 4th Avenue and Baker Street. It's right in downtown Mount Dora, and a stroll through the business district of this town will have you thinking you're in New England. There are more than a dozen antiques shops here. It's only a short walk to Lake Dora where there's a yacht club and a lakefront that's usually busy with boaters coming and going.

This route has much to offer. It starts and ends in one of the state's prettiest towns, takes you alongside Lake Dora for several miles, through some scenic rural country and up and down enough hills to make it interesting. Sugarloaf Mountain is not Pike's Peak, but it's about as good as you'll find in a state never noted for its altitude.

Sugarloaf Mountain loop

1. Turn right out of parking lot at 4th Avenue and Baker Street and go four-tenths of a mile to 11th Avenue.
2. Turn left on 11th Avenue and go eight-tenths of a mile to "Y" intersection.
3. Turn left at "Y" intersection onto Lakeshore Drive and go one-tenth of a mile to Old 441 and railroad tracks.
4. Cross Old 441 and railroad tracks and continue on

Lakeshore Drive for 4.8 miles to railroad track crossing in Tavares.

5. Cross railroad track with caution and go straight ahead on Main Street for eight-tenths of a mile to Lake Avenue.

6. Turn left on Lake Avenue and go three-tenths of a mile to Wells Avenue.

7. Turn right on Wells Avenue and go one-tenth of a mile to Mansfield Street.

8. Turn left on Mansfield, which becomes County Road, and go nine-tenths of a mile to S.R. 19.

9. Turn right on S.R. 19 and go a few yards to Birch Boulevard.

10. Turn left on Birch Boulevard and go two-tenths of a mile to Cedar Avenue.

11. Turn left on Cedar Avenue and go four-tenths of a mile to Woodlea Road, which becomes Lane Park Road.

12. Turn right on Woodlea-Lane Park Road and go 4.5 miles to C.R. 561.

13. Turn right on C.R. 561 and go 6.8 miles to C.R. 455.

14. Turn left on C.R. 455 and go 10.9 miles to where C.R. 455 turns right and crosses Florida Turnpike.

15. Turn right and go one-tenth of a mile to Old Highway 50.

16. Turn right on Old Highway 50 and go 4.2 miles to Grassy Lake Road.

17. Make sharp turn to right onto Grassy Lake Road and go 4.5 miles to C.R. 561A. Grassy Lake Road is also Rockwell for part of road. At junction where Grassy Lake Road goes straight ahead and also turns right, turn right.

18. Turn right on C.R. 561A and go 1.3 miles to Sugar-loaf Mountain Road.

19. Turn left on Sugarloaf Mountain Road and go 3.8

miles to C.R. 561.

20. Turn right on C.R. 561 and go 4.7 miles to C.R. 48.
21. Turn right on C.R. 48 and go 4.4 miles to C.R. 448A.
22. Turn left on C.R. 448A and go 1.5 miles to C.R. 448 and stop sign.
23. Turn right on C.R. 448 and go 1.3 miles to Dora Drive.
24. Turn left on Dora Drive and go 2.3 miles to Beauclair Street.
25. Turn right on Beauclair Street and go three-tenths of a mile to Clayton Street.
26. Turn left on Clayton Street and go eight-tenths of a mile to Johns Avenue.
27. Turn left on Johns Avenue and go two-tenths of a mile to Grandview Street.
28. Turn right on Grandview Street and go two-tenths of a mile to Liberty Avenue.
29. Turn left on Liberty Avenue and go one-tenth of a mile to Gilbert Park and Tremain Street.
30. Turn right on Tremain Street and go four-tenths of a mile to 4th Avenue.
31. Turn left on 4th Avenue and go one block to starting point in parking lot.

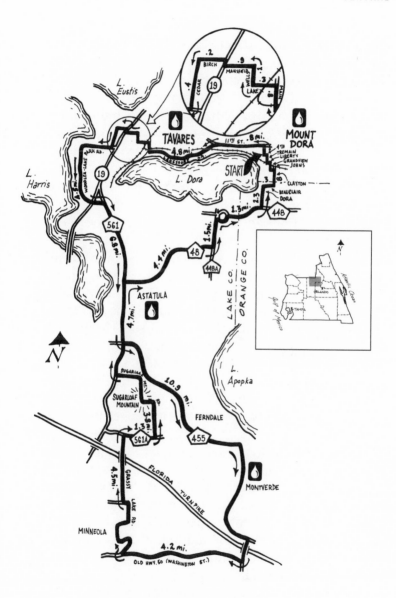

▲ Homosassa Springs-Floral City loop

This 71-mile loop through the gently rolling terrain of Citrus and Hernando counties includes stops at a state historic site and at Homosassa Springs Park.

You'll be close to areas that have grown tremendously in recent years, but this route winds through mostly rural country. Some of the hills will have you shifting to the lower gears.

After leaving the starting point at the Yulee Sugar Mill Park, you'll ride through only two towns — Homosassa Springs and Floral City, not quite the route's halfway point.

Since this is a one-day ride, the Yulee Sugar Mill Park is a good place to leave your car. There is a picnic area and room for parking. Built in 1851 by David Levy Yulee, Florida's first U.S. senator, the sugar mill now is a ruin and has been designated a state historic site. The mill was part of a 5,100-acre plantation and was used to supply the Confederate Army with sugar during the Civil War.

Less than two miles from the sugar mill ruin is the Homosassa Springs Park. Formerly Nature World, the name was changed when the state took over the attraction in 1989.

Homosassa Springs Park is one of the state's most unusual recreational adventures. The huge spring, the headwater of the beautiful Homosassa River, spews out 6 million gallons of clear water every hour. There's plenty to see and do at this park. There's a jungle cruise on a tropical waterway, alligator and hippotamus programs, manatee programs and animal encounters. Plan to spend three hours to see it all.

Visitors can go below the water's surface in the "Fish Bowl," the park's floating observatory, to see thousands

Homosassa Springs

of fresh and saltwater fish and manatees. That both fresh and saltwater fish inhabit the spring is an unexplained phenomenon. The spring also is one of the few places in the world where manatees can be observed at close range every day of the year.

If you get an early start, there will be time to complete the entire route, even after spending three hours at the park.

Shortly after leaving Homosassa Springs Park, you'll approach U.S. Highway 19-98, a busy four-lane divided highway. There's a traffic light there, so there's no problem crossing the highway. After you cross, continue on Grover Cleveland Boulevard. The road goes through some housing developments that recently have sprung up. Most of the commercial development has been along U.S. Highway 19-98.

After you leave the Homosassa Springs area, you quickly enter rural country with lots of hills to climb on County Road 480. There are lots of woods and few houses, and the scenic surroundings and good roads are fine for biking.

Just before reaching the 30-mile mark on the route, you'll come to the town of Floral City. The population now is only about 1,000, but in the first decade of the 20th century when phosphate mining created a boom in the area, Floral City had 10,000 residents. In 1885, when the population was 300, Floral City was twice the size of Miami.

The scenic highlight of the trip is in Floral City. As you leave the town on C.R. 48, you'll pass under a canopy of large oaks draped with long, hanging strands of Spanish moss. It's a spectacular sight.

The return to Homosassa Springs from Floral City is in isolated country with very little traffic. When you get on C.R. 39 soon after leaving Floral City, be careful about a fork in the road. Veer left after 1.7 miles onto Istachatta Road. That will take you into Hernando County and the settlement of Istachatta. From there you'll be heading into the Withlacoochee State Forest. This is heavily wooded country all the way back to U.S. Highway 19-98.

You'll be on C.R. 476 for about 12 miles, and some of it is fairly rough. It's not well-marked and makes several turns, but it's the only hard-surfaced road around, so you won't get lost.

There will be more than six miles on U.S. Highway 19-98 before you return to your starting point, but the traffic is not a problem. While it may be fairly heavy, there is an extra lane for four-wheel-drive vehicles and a wide, paved lane on the right for bicycles. Stay in that bicycle lane, and it's easy going the rest of the way.

As you approach C.R. 490A and the last few miles to the sugar mill ruin, you'll pass through some commercial development on U.S. Highway 19-98. There are several places along here to stop for a cold drink or a meal.

Stock up with water before leaving on this route. After Homosassa Springs there will be no place to refill your water bottles until you reach Floral City. From there it's another long stretch before you can get cold drinks or water.

If you plan to combine a visit to Homosassa Springs Park with the 71-mile ride, tour the park first. The park closes at 5:30 p.m. and doesn't sell tickets after 4 p.m. You'd be hard-pressed to see it all.

Homosassa Springs-Floral City loop

1. Turn right out of Yulee Sugar Mill Ruin picnic grounds and go 2 miles to Halls River Road (C.R. 490A).
2. Turn right on Halls River Road and go six-tenths of a mile to U.S. Highway 19-98.
3. Cross U.S. Highway 19-98 and go straight ahead on Grover Cleveland Boulevard for 5.5 miles to C.R. 491.
4. Turn right on C.R. 491 and go 9.2 miles to C.R. 480.
5. Turn left on C.R. 480 and go 5.8 miles to C.R. 581.
6. Turn left on C.R. 581 and go one-tenth of a mile to C.R. 480.
7. Turn right on C.R. 480 and go 4.3 miles to U.S. Highway 41.
8. Turn left on U.S. Highway 41 and go 1.3 miles to C.R. 48.
9. Turn right on C.R. 48 in town of Floral City and go 1.7 miles to C.R. 39.
10. Turn right on C.R. 39 and go 1.7 miles to Istachatta Road.
11. Turn left on Istachatta Road and go 5.7 miles to C.R. 476.

12. Turn right on C.R. 476 and go 5.4 miles to C.R. 581.
13. Turn right on C.R. 581 and go one-tenth of a mile to C.R. 476.
14. Turn left on C.R. 476 and go 6.2 miles to C.R. 491.
15. Turn right on C.R. 491 and go 5.5 miles to C.R. 480.
16. Turn left on C.R 480 and go 6.9 miles to U.S. Highway 19-98.
17. Turn right on U.S. Highway 19-98 and go 6.4 miles to C.R. 490A.
18. Turn left on C.R. 490A and go six-tenths of a mile to Fish Bowl Drive.
19. Turn left on Fish Bowl Drive and go 2 miles to Yulee Sugar Mill Ruin and end of route.

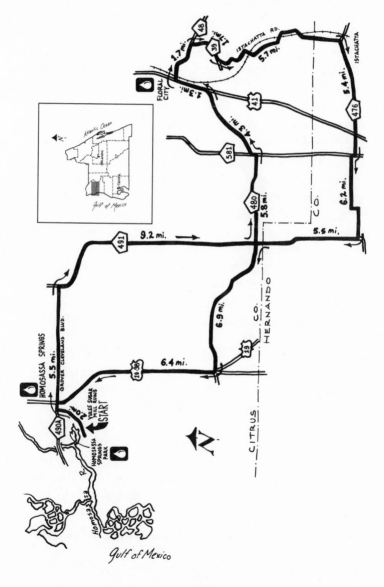

Gulf of Mexico

205

▲ Zephyrhills-Brooksville loop

If you enjoy the challenge of long and steep hills, many of the best Florida has to offer are included in this 105-mile route that begins and ends in Zephyrhills and winds through the countryside of Pasco, Hernando and Sumter counties.

This ride will have you shifting gears as you navigate some real monster hills. They start almost as soon as you leave Zephyrhills and don't end until you ride into Dade City shortly before the route's finish.

Experienced riders could manage the entire route in a single day — even with all the hills — but a two-day adventure is recommended with an overnight stop in Brooksville. There are motels and campgrounds in the Brooksville area that won't take you far off the route. With an overnight stay in Brooksville the ride breaks down to about 40 miles on the first day and a little more than 64 miles on the second day.

Pasco and Hernando counties have been among the fastest growing in Florida during the '70s and early '80s, but even with all this growth there are enough rural areas with quiet roads to make this route a delightful experience. Your only encounter with a busy road will come in Sumter and Hernando counties when you pedal 7.5 miles on U.S. Highway 301. This is a fairly busy stretch, so be sure to wear bright clothing and ride single file.

The starting point in Zephyrhills will be from a parking lot next to City Hall, across the street from the fire station. It will be at the corner of 7th Street and 6th Avenue.

Zephyrhills, with a population of about 7,000, is best-known for the fine drinking water that comes from seven of the deepest wells in Florida. A commercial firm distributes the water by trucks all over the state.

When severe freezes in 1983 and 1985 killed thousands of citrus trees in the area around the town, much of this acreage was converted to mobile home parks, and there are now 150 parks in the areas surrounding Zephyrhills.

About five miles after leaving Zephyrhills you'll be on a hill that will really impress you. That will be LeHeup Hill, and you'll need all the gears you've got. The elevation is 225 feet, and it's very long and very steep. But the view at the top is your reward. It's magnificent. Stop to catch your breath after the climb and enjoy the panorama spread below you.

From here all the way to Brooksville, it's a hilly ride. The route gets very involved just before Brooksville, so pay close attention to the directions. It's particularly confusing when you make the final turn that takes you into Brooksville.

You'll be on County Road 581, and you need to turn off this road to Mitchell Road. The turn is not well-marked. Watch for a large Jehovah's Witnesses hall on your left. Turn left there and you'll be on Mitchell Road. As you wind your way through some wooded areas and suburban developments, you'll eventually be on Main Street. This extension of Mitchell Road will take you through downtown Brooksville, past the Hernando County Courthouse.

As you get on the north side of Brooksville, Main Street becomes Howell Avenue and later dead-ends at U.S. Highway 41 on the outskirts of town.

Brooksville is the county seat of Hernando County and is the only incorporated town in the county. Its population is about 8,000, though growth outside the city has been mushrooming much faster. The elevation in

Brooksville is nearly 200 feet, and it's one of the hilliest towns in the state. Like Rome, it's built on seven hills, and you'll get acquainted with some of them as you pedal through the town.

After you turn onto U.S. Highway 41, you'll need to be especially careful crossing against traffic onto Old Crystal River Road. This road also is not well-marked, but it's about four-tenths of a mile after you enter U.S. Highway 41. From that turn it's three miles to C.R. 476.

There will be a stretch of 12 miles on C.R. 476 that will take you into Sumter County. This is wooded country with light traffic. You will turn off this road onto C.R. 476B, then ride another 7.5 miles to the previously mentioned U.S. Highway 301. The latter road runs parallel with Interstate 75, which is only about four miles west, so most of the truck traffic is on the interstate. There is still a fair amount of auto traffic on U.S. Highway 301, so stay alert.

From U.S. Highway 301 you'll turn onto S.R. 50 at the community of Ridge Manor, then ride one mile to the turn onto C.R. 575. This is a country road that will take you through the towns of Lacoochee, Trilacoochee and Trilby.

Now you can look forward to some more hill climbing as you approach Dade City. These are hills that will rival those you faced on leaving Zephyrhills, and they don't stop until you're on the outskirts of Dade City.

The route will take you past the Pasco-Hernando Community College Campus then into downtown Dade City.

Pasco is another of those counties that experienced spectacular growth during the period from 1970 to 1990, but most of this growth was in the western part of the county, mostly around New Port Richey. Dade City, the county seat, hasn't experienced that much growth, and its population is about 5,500. It's a pleasant town, and route will take you past the courthouse in the downtown area.

Caution again is advised as you make the switch from U.S. Highway 98 to C.R. 35A. You'll have to cross against the oncoming traffic to reach C.R. 35A, so be sure to signal your turn well in advance.

From 35A there will be several more twists and turns on the way back to Zephyrhills. Pay close attention to the directions from the time you get on C.R. 41 on the north side of Dade City until you reach U.S. Highway 301 in Zephyrhills.

This is a strenuous ride with lots of hills, but it's also a route that offers outstanding scenery and some really spectacular views. It's almost a roller coaster at times.

Be sure to carry plenty of water, especially on that first day. The route goes through only one town, San Antonio, between Zephyrhills and Brooksville. There are several convenience stores on the second day, but there still are some long stretches between refueling stops.

For those who may want to avoid U.S. Highway 301 (though it's not really that bad), you can take the route to Brooksville, spend the night there, then return on the same route the next day.

Of course, if you don't mind 80 miles of hills, ride to Brooksville and back on the same day.

Zephyrhills-Brooksville loop
1. Turn right out of parking lot on 7th Street and go seven-tenths of a mile to North Avenue.
2. Turn left on North Avenue and go one block to Fort King Road.
3. Turn right on Fort King Road and go 6.5 miles to C.R. 52A.

4. Turn left on C.R. 52A and go 2 miles to C.R. 579.

5. Turn left on C.R. 579 and go 3.9 miles to C.R. 577.

6. Go straight on C.R. 577 for 4.2 miles to where C.R. 577 turns.

7. Turn left on C.R. 577 and go one-half of a mile to C.R. 577 and C.R. 578.

8. Turn left on C.R. 577 and C.R. 578 and go one-half of a mile to C.R. 577.

9. Turn right on C.R. 577 and go 4.6 miles to C.R. 41, which becomes C.R. 541 after crossing into Hernando County.

10. Go straight ahead on C.R. 541 for 3.5 miles to C.R. 576.

11. Turn left on C.R. 576 and go 5.3 miles to C.R. 581.

12. Turn right on C.R. 581 and go 3 miles to junction with C.R. 572.

13. Turn right on C.R. 581 and go one-half of a mile to junction with C.R. 572.

14. Turn left at junction with C.R. 572 on C.R. 581 and go 2.2 miles to Mitchell Road at Jehovah's Witnesses hall.

15. Turn left on Mitchell Road at hall and go 4.4 miles to U.S. Highway 41 north of Brooksville. Mitchell Road becomes Main Street in Brooksville, then becomes Howell Avenue.

16. Turn left on U.S. Highway 41 and go four-tenths of a mile to Old Crystal River Road.

17. Turn left on Old Crystal River Road and go 3 miles to C.R. 476.

18. Turn right on C.R. 476 and go 12 miles to C.R. 476B.

19. Turn right on C.R. 476B and go 7.5 miles to U.S. Highway 301.

20. Turn right on U.S. Highway 301 and go 7.5 mile to S.R. 50.

21. Turn left on S.R. 50 and go 1 mile to C.R. 575.

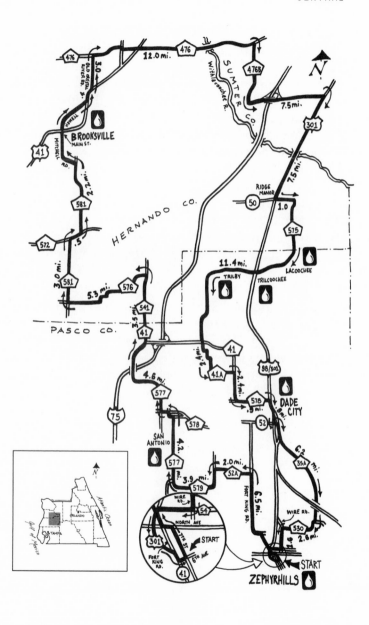

22. Turn right on C.R. 575 and go 11.4 miles to C.R. 41A.
23. Go straight on C.R. 41A and go 2.4 miles to C.R. 41.
24. Turn right on C.R. 41 and go 2.4 miles to C.R. 578.
25. Go straight ahead on C.R. 578 and go nine-tenths of a mile to U.S. Highway 98 and U.S. Highway 301 in Dade City.
26. Turn right on U.S. Highway 98 and U.S. Highway 301 and go eight-tenths of a mile to S.R. 52.
27. Turn left on S.R. 52 and go three-tenths of a mile to U.S. Highway 98.
28. Turn right on U.S. Highway 98 and go two-tenths of a mile to C.R. 35A.
29. Turn left on C.R. 35A and go 6.2 miles to C.R. 530.
30. Go straight ahead on C.R. 530 for 2.6 miles to Wire Road.
31. Turn left on Wire Road and go 1.6 miles to C.R. 54.
32. Turn right on C.R. 54 and go one-half of a mile to U.S. Highway 301.
33. Turn left on U.S. Highway 301 and go 1.4 miles to 6th Avenue in Zephyrhills.
34. Turn left on 6th Avenue and go one block to parking lot and end of route.

4. South

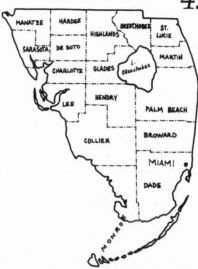

▲ Arcadia-Myakka River State Park loop

Down in the middle of South Florida's cattle country is the Myakka River State Park with 28,875 acres that have remained virtually unchanged for centuries. It's the overnight stopping point for a two-day ride that begins in Arcadia.

This ride takes you through De Soto, Sarasota, Manatee and Hardee counties. The first day's trip covers 37 miles; the second leg of the journey is 60 miles.

Myakka is Florida's largest state park. It's famous for outstanding scenery with great panoramas of lakes, streams, marshes, hammocks and prairies. Wildlife is abundant.

The area where the park is located was discovered centuries ago by a small band of Myaca Indians. They enjoyed the plentiful game and birds, the abundance of fish in the lakes and streams and the moist and fertile soil. The Indians were forced out of this paradise by the white man, and while the spelling was changed to Myakka, the original pronunciation was retained.

Camping facilities with restrooms and showers are available at two locations in the park. There also are five rustic cabins that can be rented.

A seven-mile long road winds its way through the park and will give bikers an excellent chance to see this beautiful subtropical setting and the many species of wading birds and waterfowl that flock here in the winter. Ospreys, bald eagles and sandhill cranes are common then.

An interpretive center has exhibits of wildlife and plants found in the park and a slide program.

The park rangers provide guided walks and campfire programs at various times of the year. During the winter they offer bird watching programs for beginners.

There also are boat tours of Upper Myakka Lake and tram tours of the hardwood hammock and the river flood plain on a seasonal basis.

During your stay in the park you might want to check the wilderness preserve. This 7,500-acre area resembles Florida before the white man's arrival. A limited number of visitors are allowed to visit this preserve each day on foot or by boat.

Cyclists should be advised that the north entrance to the park is closed on weekdays and open only on Saturdays, Sundays and holidays. This doesn't mean you can't get through that padlocked entrance on weekdays — but it involves lifting your bike and gear over the fence. Quite a few riders do this.

Your starting point for this loop is at a city parking lot across the street from the Arcadia police station.

Myakka River State Park

You'll exit onto State Road 70, then ride a couple of miles on that road before turning onto S.R. 72 and heading west toward Myakka. This will be a stretch of more than 28 miles, and most of it is through cattle pastures. That's the major agricultural interest in this area, though citrus and vegetable growing also are profitable.

Arcadia is the county seat of De Soto County and the only incorporated town in the county. It has experienced very little growth, and its population remains steady at about 6,000.

De Soto County originally was part of Hillsborough County and later became part of Manatee County. It was created from Manatee in 1887 and was named for the Spanish explorer, Hernando De Soto. In 1921 De Soto was subdivided into five counties — De Soto, Glades, Hardee, Highlands and Charlotte.

In its early years, Arcadia was considered one of Florida's wildest towns because of a series of cattle wars in which many lives were lost over cattle rustling.

Frederic Remington, the famous cowboy painter, completed a series of paintings based on Arcadia during this period.

Traffic on S.R. 72 is light, so you should enjoy a quiet ride to Myakka. As you get within a few miles of the park, the landscape will change. You'll leave cattle country and get into heavily wooded areas that will continue right up to the park entrance.

After you leave Myakka you'll have about five miles of quiet roads before reaching S.R. 70. This is a fairly busy east-west highway; be sure to wear brightly colored clothing and ride single file.

The ride on S.R. 70 ends at the community of Myakka City. There are a couple of stores here and a few houses, and it will be a good place to refill your water bottles.

From Myakka City the route heads north on Wauchula Road. This is a smooth road, but you'll be in for a surprise when you get to the last three miles. The quiet two-lane highway suddenly ends, becoming a single-lane road. Motorists using this road solve the problem of meeting oncoming cars by getting partially off the road. Fortunately the traffic is so light it will not pose a problem for bikers.

This unique one-lane road ends at S.R. 64, and you'll be on that for almost 14 miles before heading south again toward Arcadia on County Road 661 in Hardee County. The traffic here is very light for almost 20 miles before reaching S.R. 70 and the final leg into Arcadia.

You might get a little confused after the first four miles on C.R. 661. The road curves to the right, then about two-tenths of a mile later you reach what is marked as Murphy Road S.W. Turn left there and continue to the community of Limestone. There's a store there. Refill your water bottles here. At this point the road is marked

Central Avenue S.W. It's also C.R. 661, the road you take back to S.R. 70.

The 20-mile stretch between S.R. 64 and S.R. 70 has two hazards that could cause trouble. Two single-lane bridges are surfaced with wooden boards. Be careful in riding across these old bridges to avoid getting your wheels caught between those boards.

Except for the nine miles on S.R. 70 after you leave Myakka River State Park, this is a ride over quiet roads through sparsely populated, rural country.

Myakka River State Park is the real highlight of this ride, and those who try to crowd all 97 miles into a single day will be passing up a chance to explore what is certainly one of Florida's most beautiful state parks.

Arcadia-Myakka River State Park loop

1. Exit parking lot at corner of Hickory Street and Polk Avenue onto Hickory Street (S.R. 70) and go 1.8 miles to S.R. 72.
2. Turn left on S.R. 72 and go 28.3 miles to Myakka River State Park.
3. Go straight ahead on park road for 7 miles to north entrance to park.
4. Go straight ahead after leaving park on Myakka Road for 3.7 miles to Verna Road.
5. Go straight ahead on Verna Road for 1.4 miles to S.R. 70.
6. Turn right on S.R. 70 and go 9.3 miles to Carlton Avenue in Myakka City.
7. Turn left on Carlton Avenue, then right and go two-tenths of a mile to Wauchula Road.
8. Turn left on Wauchula Road and go 10.3 miles to S.R. 64.
9. Turn right on S.R. 64 and go 13.9 miles to C.R. 661.

10. Turn right on C.R. 661 and go 4.2 miles to Murphy Road S.W.
11. Turn left on Murphy Road S.W. and go 5.2 miles to Central Avenue S.W. in Limestone.
12. Turn left on Central Avenue S.W. and go one block to where Central Avenue curves and becomes C.R. 661.
13. Go straight on Central Avenue S.W. (C.R. 661) for 9.7 miles to S.R. 70 near Arcadia.
14. Turn left on S.R. 70 and go 1.3 miles to where road curves, going straight ahead on West Oak Street into Historic Business District.
15. Go straight on Oak Street for eight-tenths of a mile to Polk Avenue.
16. Turn left on Polk Avenue and go one block to parking lot and end of route.

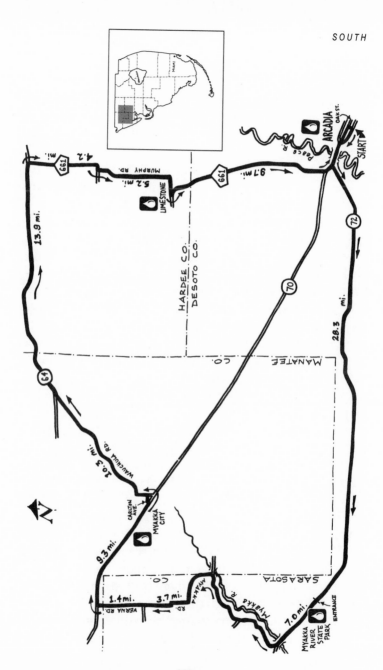

▲ Lakeland-Arcadia loop

This meandering loop starts in the heart of Florida's citrus belt in Lakeland and travels to the cattle country of South Florida through Polk, Hardee and De Soto counties. It's about 144 miles.

This two-day ride has an overnight stop scheduled for Arcadia — 69 miles from Lakeland. The return journey will be about 75 miles.

Be sure to keep your directions close at hand on this loop. There are more than 60 turns and changes of routes.

Though it's involved, this is an interesting loop. From Lakeland the ride heads south through citrus groves, through the phosphate mining region of Polk County, back into orange and grapefruit groves, and finally into the cattle ranches surrounding Arcadia.

Lakeland's population is about 60,000, and it is one of the three largest inland cities in Florida. With 13 lakes in the city limits, the place is aptly named. Citrus groves surround Lakeland. Shipping and processing fruit are major industries.

This route is the only one in the book that starts from a major city, but don't let that disturb you.

You'll be starting from the Southgate Shopping Center on Florida Avenue. This is on the south side of Lakeland, and you'll have only a little more than a mile on Florida Avenue, State Road 37. From there you quickly will be in the rural areas and heading toward Mulberry.

The shopping center is a safe place to leave your car overnight. It's so safe, in fact, that many Lakeland residents were leaving their cars there for indefinite periods with "for sale" signs on them. The lot finally got so crowded that signs were posted warning people not to do this for extended periods. You won't have trouble, though, if it's just for the night you'll be in Arcadia.

On your overnight stay in Arcadia you'll have a choice between three motels and an excellent KOA campground on the Peace River that's two miles out of town on the route. It's at the junction of S.R. 70 and County Road 661.

Arcadia is in an area of Florida that has experienced very little growth. Cattle is the major agricultural interest here. Half of the residents in De Soto county are lifelong Floridians, and the population in Arcadia has stayed around 6,000 for several years.

After winding through the suburban areas of Lakeland and down four-laned S.R. 37 into Mulberry, the route will head into some rather unusual-looking country. Mulberry bills itself as the world's phosphate center.

About 70 percent of the world's phosphate, the chief ingredient in fertilizer, is mined in the Lakeland area, and Mulberry is always associated with phosphate.

Until fairly recently, much of the countryside around this area resembled a moonscape. Years of phosphate mining had left large piles of debris and gaping craters. During the past 20 years, steps have been taken to reverse the damage. The piles of debris have been leveled, and many of the holes have been filled with dirt and seeded with grass.

Phosphate still is big here, though discoveries of it have been made in so many other parts of the world that production here has lagged lately. From the Mulberry area south for many miles you'll be pedaling through phosphate country. It will change to citrus as you get into Hardee County.

Two miles south of S.R. 60 in Mulberry, be extra careful as you switch from S.R. 37 to Old 37. Veer left onto

Old 37, and you'll cross a lane of oncoming traffic; indicate that left turn well in advance. After you get on Old 37 you need to watch for two turns. The first is in the abandoned town of Pierce, where you make a sharp turn right after about two miles. Three miles later you'll be in Bradley, and Old 37 makes another left turn here, though it's not well-marked. There will be a store on your right as you make the turn.

You will have several involved twists and turns as you enter Hardee County, then more of the same as the route gets close to Wauchula. This is the county seat of Hardee County. Watch closely for the road signs that are indicated in your directions.

After you reach C.R. 661, which is also marked as Murphy Road on several signs, it will be easy to find your way to Arcadia. You'll arrive on the west side of the town, then have less than two miles on S.R. 70 into downtown Arcadia.

Your route out of Arcadia the next morning will put you on quiet streets on the east side of the city. There will be several changes of routes before reaching U.S. Highway 17, and you'll be on that road for a little more than a mile. The route then turns off U.S. Highway 17 onto Brownville Road. After two miles the road suddenly narrows from two lanes to a single lane for two miles. It's a lightly traveled road; you should have no problems.

From the Brownville Road you'll return to the same C.R. 661 that you were on during the first day of this route. It also is labeled Murphy Road on some of the road signs, and it eventually will bring you back to S.R. 64. From here you'll switch to C.R. 64A, then ride 5.4 miles on this to C.R. 35B. You'll again wind your way through the outskirts of Wauchula and be back on the same route you followed in the ride from Lakeland to Arcadia.

In a short distance you'll be switching from orange groves and other farmland to the phosphate mining area. There will be a stretch of five miles along C.R. 663 as you enter the phosphate country that's a notorious example of land abuse. Hundreds of piles of debris have been left over from mining operations through the years. Rainwater has collected in the great holes in the ground where the phosphate was removed, and it makes for a very strange landscape. It gets better.

The road you'll travel after leaving C.R. 664 and heading into the phosphate region will be very quiet with only an occasional mining truck sharing the road with you. There are several plants along the route and a couple of railroad track crossings where caution is advised. On both of these you'll have a sharp turn, then railroad tracks and another sharp turn in a different direction.

Some of the road markings are not good; keep a close eye on the directions. When you reach the town of Bradley, the road dead ends and is marked Main Street. Turn right there, go three miles to another dead end and turn left.

After this final turn you'll have a short ride to where Old 37 merges into S.R. 37. Watch out for this one as you did on the first day. Fast-moving traffic will be coming toward you on your left. From here it's less than two miles to Mulberry. After you cross S.R. 60 in Mulberry, the road becomes a divided four-lane highway, and you'll stay on that all the way to the next traffic light, Shepherd Road.

Turn left on Shepherd Road and follow the same route you took on leaving Lakeland.

This is a route that is recommended for a weekend, since it starts and finishes in a large city. If you confine your riding to Saturday and Sunday you should have no problems.

The toughest part of this ride is the constant changing of routes. It would be a good idea to study the directions closely before leaving, then refer to them repeatedly throughout the trip. On the return trip you'll be riding on many of the same roads you coped with on the first day. Before leaving Arcadia, check the map and directions from there until you pick up the first day's route near Wauchula.

Aside from the miles through the phosphate mining region, this is a loop through pleasant rural areas over good roads that have very little traffic.

This also is another of those routes where you need to start with a full water bottle and fill it at every opportunity. There are several stretches where you'll have many miles between refueling stops, so it's advisable to carry two bottles with you.

Lakeland-Arcadia loop

1. Exit right out of Southgate Shopping Center on South Florida Avenue and go 1.1 miles to C.R. 572 (Drane Field Road).
2. Turn right on C.R. 572 and go three-tenths of a mile to Old 37.
3. Turn left on Old 37 and go 1.5 miles to dead end.
4. Turn right at dead end on West Pipkin Road and go eight-tenths of a mile to Old 37.
5. Turn left on Old 37 and go 2.6 miles to Shepherd Road.
6. Turn left on Shepherd Road and go one-tenth of a mile to S.R. 37.
7. Turn right on S.R. 37 and go 5.2 miles to Old 37.
8. Veer left on Old 37 and go 2.2 miles to where Old 37 turns right.

9. Turn right on Old 37 and go 3.1 miles to where road turns left in Bradley.

10. Turn left on Old 37 and go 3 miles to where road turns.

11. Turn right, cross railroad tracks, then turn left and continue for six-tenths of a mile to C.R. 630.

12. Cross C.R. 630. (Road name changes to Fort Green Road.) Go straight ahead on Fort Green Road for 4.1 miles to where road turns right.

13. Turn right, cross railroad tracks, then turn left.

14. Go straight ahead after turn for 5 miles to C.R. 664.

15. Turn left on C.R. 664 and go 4.7 miles to College Hill Road.

16. Turn right on College Hill Road and go 2.3 miles to S.R. 62.

17. Turn left on S.R. 62; go 1.5 miles to Polk Road N.W.

18. Turn right on Polk Road N.W. and go 2.6 miles to Terrell Road.

19. Turn right on Terrell Road and go 1.3 miles to C.R. 64A.

20. Turn right on C.R. 64A and go 5.4 miles to S.R. 64.

21. Turn right on S.R. 64 and go two-tenths of a mile to C.R. 661.

22. Turn left on C.R. 661 and go 4 miles to curve.

23. Turn right on curve and go two-tenths of a mile to Murphy Road.

24. Turn left on Murphy Road and go 5.2 miles to Central Avenue S.W. in Limestone.

25. Turn left on Central Avenue S.W. and go one block to C.R. 661.

26. Go straight on C.R. 661 for 9.7 miles to S.R. 70.

27. Turn left on S.R. 70 and go 2.2 miles to U.S. Highway 17 in downtown Arcadia.

28. To resume route the next day, turn right on U.S. Highway 17 and go to first street past Best Western

Motel, which is Palm Avenue.

29. Turn left on Palm Avenue and go two-tenths of a mile to South Arcadia Avenue.
30. Turn left on South Arcadia Avenue and go one-tenth of a mile to Hargrave Street.
31. Turn right on Hargrave Street and go nine-tenths of a mile to Florida Avenue.
32. Turn left on Florida Avenue and go three-tenths of a mile to S.R. 70.
33. Turn right on S.R. 70 and go one-tenth of a mile to Turner Road.
34. Turn left on Turner Road and go 3.3 miles to C.R. 660.
35. Turn right on C.R. 660. The road jogs left, then right. Go 2.7 miles to C.R. 660.
36. Turn left on C.R. 660 and go six-tenths of a mile to U.S. Highway 17.
37. Turn right on U.S. Highway 17 and go 1.3 miles to Brownville Road.
38. Turn left on Brownville Road and go 4.1 miles to C.R. 661.
39. Turn right on C.R. 661 and go 4.6 miles to Central Avenue in Limestone.
40. Go straight on Central Avenue for one block to Murphy Road N.W.
41. Turn right on Murphy Road and go 5.3 miles to turn in road.
42. Turn right on Murphy Road N.W. and go two-tenths of a mile to Murphy Road.
43. Turn left on Murphy Road and go 4 miles to S.R. 64.
44. Turn right on S.R. 64 and go two-tenths of a mile to C.R. 64A.
45. Turn left on C.R. 64A and go 5.4 miles to C.R. 35B.
46. Turn left on C.R. 35B and go 1.3 miles to C.R. 35B N.W.
47. Turn left on C.R. 35B N.W. (later becomes Polk

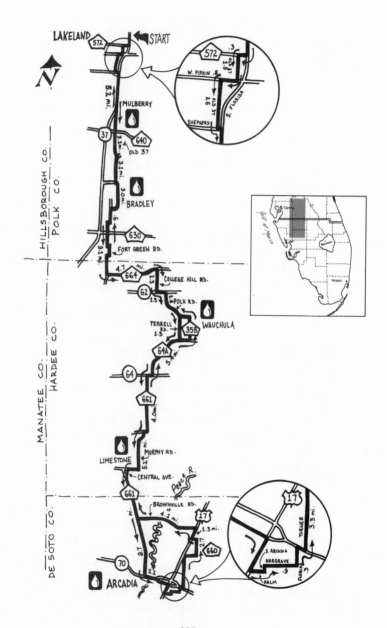

Road N.W.) and go 2.6 miles to S.R. 62.

48. Turn left on S.R. 62 and go 1.5 miles to College Hill Road.

49. Turn right on College Hill Road and go 2.3 miles to C.R. 664.

50. Turn left on C.R. 664 and go 4.7 miles to C.R. 663 (Fort Green Road).

51. Turn right on C.R. 663 and go 5 miles to where road turns, crosses tracks, then turns left.

52. Go straight after turning left for seven-tenths of a mile to Mills Road, turn left, cross tracks and continue on Fort Green Road.

53. Go straight for 3.3 miles to C.R. 630, cross it and Fort Green Road becomes Old 37.

54. Go straight on Old 37 for eight-tenths of a mile to where road turns right; cross tracks, turn left and continue on Old 37.

55. Go straight on Old 37 for 3 miles to Main Street in Bradley.

56. Turn right on Main Street and continue on Old 37 for 3.1 miles to dead end.

57. Turn left at dead end and go 2.2 miles to S.R. 37.

58. Merge into S.R. 37, go through town of Mulberry and go 5.3 miles to Shepherd Road (traffic light).

59. Turn left on Shepherd Road and go one-tenth of a mile to Old 37.

60. Turn right on Old 37 and go 2.6 miles to Pipkin Road.

61. Turn right on Pipkin Road and go eight-tenths of a mile to Old 37.

62. Turn left on Old 37 and go 1.5 miles to Drane Field Road (C.R. 572).

63. Turn right on Drane Field Road and go three-tenths of a mile to S.R. 37.

64. Turn left on S.R. 37 and go 1.1 miles to Southgate Shopping Center and end of route.

▲ *Lake Okeechobee loop*

If you're looking for a change of pace from the lakes, hills and woods of North and Central Florida, a two-day ride around Lake Okeechobee should suit you.

Changes in landscape are dramatic in this exploration of South Florida. Instead of orange groves and oak trees, you'll ride through fields of sugar cane and royal palms. No more forested hills — some of the flattest land on earth surrounds Lake Okeechobee, and it stretches from horizon to horizon.

Lake Okeechobee is the second largest freshwater lake in the United States. Only Lake Michigan is larger. Five counties border it, and this 125-mile ride will take you through all of them.

This area and the sections of Florida north of it are two different worlds. South Florida offers little exciting scenery, but it is so different from the rest of the state that a ride around this giant lake is fascinating.

The ride starts and ends in the town of Okeechobee, on the lake's north side. The name is derived from the Seminole Indian words "Oki," meaning water, and "Chobee," meaning big.

In the late 19th century, Okeechobee's chief businesses were cattle, sawmills and catfish camps by the lake. Today the town's population is almost 10,000.

Fishing is still big business here, though, and the fingerling catfish from the lake is a delicacy savored by Floridians and visitors. Truck farms supply much of the winter vegetables for the rest of the United States, and sugar cane also is a major crop.

In September 1928, the town of Okeechobee suffered the worst natural disaster in the state's history. After devastating Puerto Rico, a hurricane headed for the mainland and crashed into Florida's lower east coast with winds of 160 mph. Radio reception in those days was poor, and Okeechobee's townspeople weren't warned of the impending storm. The hurricane took aim for Okeechobee, and when it hit, the water from the lake was driven north, flooding the town and drowning many people. Once the eye of the hurricane passed, the winds came from the opposite direction, forcing the lake's water back into the south end. Water surged through the small retaining dikes at the lake's southern shore; thousands of people drowned.

Though the final death toll was placed at about 2,400, the actual count was not known. Many of the dead were migrant workers from the Bahamas, and they couldn't be identified. The bodies of the drowned victims were burned because the land was too flooded to bury them.

Disaster struck again in 1947. After several years of drought, rain arrived and the fertile Everglades were brimming over with swirling water that covered an area twice the size of New Jersey. Thousands of people were driven from their homes, and damage for that season totaled $59 million. There was a great black sheet of water 40 miles wide flowing out of the Kissimmee Valley from Lake Okeechobee to the sloughs and from the prairies to the north. Devastation even hit the coastal communities of Palm Beach, Broward and Dade counties.

After all this damage, the U.S. Army Corps of Engineers intervened to solve the problem with the establishment of the Central and South Florida Flood Control Project in 1948. A network of canals, dikes, spillways and dams was built to crisscross the 18 counties stretching from south of Orlando to the southern tip of the Florida mainland. It worked. When monstrous Hurricane Donna swept across Florida in 1960, and when 40 inches of rain

Photograph by John Raoux/The Orlando Sentinel

Sugar cane harvesting

fell on South Florida in 1968, flood damage was minimal and no lives were lost.

Now these fertile muckland counties around Lake Okeechobee supply much of the nation's sugar and a large share of its winter vegetable crop. Millions of acres of land are devoted to farming.

Start at the City Hall in Okeechobee. There's a large parking lot and the police station is next door. The route follows U.S. Highway 441-98 for almost 35 miles as you start circling the lake. Though there's traffic as you get out of Okeechobee, the road is mostly four-laned, and there's a wide shoulder lane for bicycles when you reach the rural areas. This lane continues all the way to Martin County, the 15-mile point of the loop.

The route follows the lake almost the entire way, and in the early stages you see the big protective dikes that surround it. They'll be on your right. After 26 miles of the ride you'll finally get a good view of the lake from the highway.

As you enter Palm Beach County the shoulder lane resumes, although the traffic is not heavy enough to present a problem.

Long before you enter Palm Beach County, you'll be in sugar cane country. The huge fields extend as far as you can see.

As you enter Palm Beach County, stately, tall royal palms will appear — quite a change from the smaller varieties of palms that dot the landscape north of here.

In the town of Canal Point the route changes from U.S. Highway 441-98 to U.S. Highway 441 with U.S. Highway 98 heading southeast. In a few more miles you'll come to the town of Pahokee. This is a farming community, and large numbers of migrant workers live here while the sugar cane and winter vegetables are being harvested. There also is a state park and another good opportunity to catch a view of the lake.

The route skirts the town of Belle Glade on County Road 715 before you'll ride a few miles on State Road 80 and U.S. Highway 27. Less than three miles after you turn onto U.S. Highway 27, there will be an unmarked road on your left. It's suggested you take this road to avoid some fairly heavy traffic on U.S. Highway 27. Heavy vehicles hauling sugar cane have left this road in an undulating condition, but it's usable for bicycle traffic. The surface is not rough, but the undulations may bother you. If so, there's a road that will return you to U.S. Highway 27 after a couple of miles. This unmarked road has some stretches that are quite smooth, and the entire length of it is 7.7 miles. When you do return to U.S. Highway 27, you're in the outskirts of Clewiston.

You're in Hendry County now, another major sugar producing county. Clewiston is a town of almost 5,000 population, and it is recommended as a stopping point for the first day of your two-day ride. The U.S. Sugar Corp. has a large plant here, and it's a pleasant town with good motels and restaurants.

After leaving Clewiston you'll turn onto C.R. 720. It's the first paved road after Clewiston — it's unmarked on U.S. Highway 27. A mile later you'll enter Glades County. You're leaving the sugar cane fields behind you and trading the view for one of fields of winter vegetables, cattle and dairy farms.

Glades County is one of the least populated counties in the state. The 1980 census recorded 5,992 residents. Its county seat is Moore Haven, the only incorporated town in the county, and it has the distinction of being the first town in the United States to elect a woman mayor. You pass through there just before you turn onto S.R. 78 for the last leg of the trip.

About 12 miles after leaving Moore Haven, you'll find a store at the settlement of Lakeport. A few miles after that there's a road leading off S.R. 78 onto C.R. 721 to the Brighton Seminole Indian Reservation. This is a ride of about six miles each way, but the trip is worthwhile.

It's about 20 miles from the road leading to the Indian reservation to Okeechobee. After you visit the Indian reservation, return to S.R. 78 via C.R. 721. When you cross the Kissimmee River you're back in Okeechobee County and will retrace your steps for the last three miles back to City Hall.

As you pedal through this flat country with all its agricultural riches, it's not difficult to imagine what a challenge this swampy area must have been to the early settlers. The Seminole Indians were the only residents until well into the 19th century.

Not until 1837 did Col. Zachary Taylor lead a military campaign into this uncharted country. He left the Tampa Bay area with 2,000 men, 80 wagons and 200 pack mules and set off down the west bank of the Kissimmee River. En route, Taylor learned from captured Indians that the river continued until it reached a large lake — Okeechobee. On Christmas Day in 1887, Taylor and his troops fought the Seminole Indians near where the town of Okeechobee now is located. Taylor later became the twelfth president of the United States — partly because of his success in Florida.

This is an interesting loop. It exposes you to a portion of Florida that tourists seldom see. There's not much scenery, but the vastness of the great fields of sugar cane, vegetables and cattle are impressive.

It's not a difficult ride. The terrain is flat throughout,

and the roads are good. It's about 67 miles from Okeechobee to Clewiston, so your second day's trip will have about 58 miles if you don't include the Indian reservation, 69 miles if you do include it.

Lake Okeechobee loop

1. Turn left out of City Hall and go two-tenths of a mile to 4th Street.
2. Turn right on 4th Street and go two-tenths of a mile to Parrott Avenue (U.S. Highway 441-98).
3. Turn left on Parrott Avenue and go 2.9 miles to traffic light where U.S. Highway 441-98 turns.
4. Turn left on U.S. Highway 441-98 and go 32 miles to town of Canal Point, where U.S. Highway 441-98 becomes two separate highways.
5. Turn right on U.S. Highway 441 (U.S. Highway 98 goes straight) and go 3.5 miles to C.R. 715.
6. Turn left on U.S. Highway 441 and C.R. 715, then right on C.R. 715 and go 12.3 miles to S.R. 80.
7. Turn right on S.R. 80 and go 1.8 miles to U.S. Highway 27.
8. Turn right on U.S. Highway 27 and go 2.8 miles to unmarked road.
9. Turn left on unmarked road and go 7.7 miles to U.S. Highway 27.
10. Turn left on U.S. Highway 27 and go 8.5 miles to C.R. 720, first paved road to right after leaving town of Clewiston.
11. Turn right on C.R. 720 and go 10.5 miles to U.S. Highway 27.
12. Turn right on U.S. Highway 27 and go 3.8 miles to S.R. 78.
13. Turn right on S.R. 78 and go 34.9 miles to junction with U.S. Highway 441-98 in town of Okeechobee.

(Take C.R. 721 off of S.R. 78 to go to the Indian reservation.)

14. Turn left on U.S. Highway 441-98 and go 2.9 miles to 4th Street.
15. Turn right on 4th Street and go two-tenths of a mile to Third Avenue.
16. Turn left on Third Avenue and go two-tenths of a mile to City Hall and end of ride.

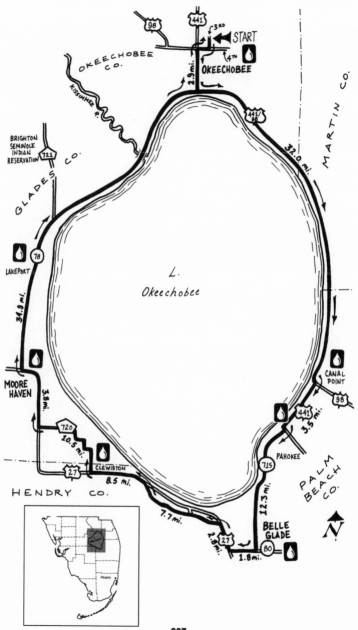

SOUTH

OKEECHOBEE CO.

OKEECHOBEE R.

KISSIMMEE R.

BRIGHTON
SEMINOLE
INDIAN
RESERVATION — 721

GLADES CO.

98

441

3RD

START

4TH

OKEECHOBEE

2.9 mi.

441/98

32.0 mi.

MARTIN CO.

78

LAKEPORT

34.9 mi.

L.
Okeechobee

CANAL
POINT

98

MOORE
HAVEN

3.8 mi.

720

10.5 mi.

27

CLEWISTON

8.5 mi.

441

3.5 mi.

PAHOKEE

715

12.3 mi.

HENDRY CO.

7.7 mi.

2.8 mi.

27

PALM
BEACH
CO.

BELLE
GLADE

80

1.8 mi.

MIAMI

N

▲ Mulberry-Sebring loop

Some of the largest citrus groves in Florida and one of the state's biggest mining operations are included in this 130-mile ride through Polk, Hardee and Highlands counties. It begins and ends in Mulberry, with an overnight stop in Sebring.

There is a variety of scenery on this route, but it's all flat terrain. The first day's ride covers 67 miles; the second day has 63 miles.

The loop takes you past the Kenilworth Lodge in Sebring, which would be a convenient spot to spend the night. There also are several hotels in Sebring, and Highlands Hammock State Park is about four miles west of town. The park is a 3,800-acre wilderness of luxuriant vegetation, dense jungle, swamps and pools. It's a delightful place to camp. Getting to the park — and then back to where the ride resumes the next morning — is not difficult.

Park your car in the lot behind the Mulberry City Hall at the corner of State Road 60 and S.R. 37. Head south on S.R. 37.

Mulberry, with a population of about 4,500, describes itself as the world's phosphate center. You'll realize this is hardly an exaggeration as you pedal your way through the vast mining operations between Mulberry and Hardee County.

Mulberry's history is unique. In its early days, the town was sparsely populated, and the longleaf yellow pine trees made logging the principal industry. The town had no name, but train crews left passengers and mail at a mulberry tree beside the railroad tracks.

In 1886 phosphate ore was discovered at the mouth of the Peace River, and the quiet little town suddenly was booming. Railroad shipments increased, but goods still were marked to be put off at the mulberry tree. As the town grew, a railroad station was built by the tree. The city's name, quite naturally, was Mulberry.

As the city boomed, so did the lawlessness. Every man carried firearms. Lynchings and shootings became common, and legend has it that many a lynch mobs' noose hung from the mulberry tree.

Though the tree survived for more than 100 years, it finally had to be replaced. The new mulberry tree is near city hall.

Mulberry, six miles south of Lakeland, is considerably quieter than it was in those boisterous early years. Phosphate dominates the scene, and you'll be into the mining country almost as soon as you leave the city limits.

Be careful when you switch from S.R. 37 onto Old 37 about two miles south of Mulberry. You'll have to cross in front of a lane of oncoming traffic to veer left onto Old 37.

Just two miles after you turn onto Old 37 you'll come to a sharp turn to the right. You're now at the spot where the town of Pierce used to be. Up until shortly after World War II, Pierce was a busy town with more than 100 houses and several businesses — all owned by a phosphate company. When the phosphate was mined out, the town shut down; the buildings were dismantled, and now only a large grassy tract is in the area where Pierce had flourished.

You'll be in phosphate country from the start of Old 37 all the way to Hardee County. It's not scenic, but this region has produced millions of tons of phosphate, the chief ingredient in fertilizers.

The landscape for the next 16 miles is marred in many places by large piles of mining debris and by gaping holes where the phosphate was extracted. These giant craters have filled with rain through the years. Mining companies recently have tried to improve the terrain and have smoothed out many of the piles and planted grass — it's much better than it used to be.

The route passes over several railroad crossings, and many of the crossings are rough.

Pay close attention to the directions — road numbers change frequently, and the route twists and turns.

When you leave the phosphate area and head east on County Road 664, you'll be in citrus country; groves will line the highway. The route travels on quiet roads with little traffic all the way to Sebring. You'll pass close to Wauchula, but the only town on the route before Sebring is Zolfo Springs.

In Zolfo Springs be alert for Myrtle Street. It's the last street before you reach U.S. Highway 17, which is busy at this point. Turn right on Myrtle Street and follow it across S.R. 66.

There's a stretch of 23 miles on S.R. 66 after Zolfo Springs that will bring you to Sebring's outskirts.

Sebring fronts Lake Jackson. Its population is close to 10,000, and another 35,000 are living just outside the city limits.

Rolling hills covered with citrus groves surround Sebring. The town is best-known for hosting the annual International Grand Prix Sports Car 12-hour Endurance Race in March. Sebring bulges with crowds of more than 50,000 for that event; don't plan a bike trip during that week.

Founded in 1912 by George Sebring, an Ohio ceramic manufacturer, the town has impressive residential and business sections. The route will take you through many of these sections.

Pay attention to the directions as you pedal your way out of town. It's a twisting route that will bring you into another South Florida town, Avon Park. You'll ride past a milelong mall there that showcases more than 1,000 varieties of trees, plants and shrubs.

After riding past the mall, you'll be in rural country and will make several route changes before riding through Fort Meade. From there you'll have more than 10 miles on C.R. 640, then three more miles into Mulberry and the end of the route.

This route is full of turns — 47 of them. Some are not well-marked. Keep your eye on the directions.

The variety of scenery — the phosphate mining at the ride's start and the miles of citrus — makes this an interesting ride. But the highlight of the loop is Sebring. It's a delightful place. Take some time to look around. The downtown area, built around an oak tree in the middle of a park, is good for browsing. Founder Sebring planned this area with the streets spread like spokes of a wheel around the park.

Neither day's ride is difficult. The roads are quiet and in good condition. Though you will pass through only a few small towns, water shouldn't be a problem. There are some convenience stores, and there are farmhouses along the route after you clear the phosphate section.

Mulberry-Sebring loop
1. Turn left out of parking lot behind City Hall onto S.R. 37 and go 2.2 miles to where Old 37 veers left.
2. Go straight on Old 37 for 2.2 miles to where Old 37 turns right.
3. Turn right on Old 37 and go 3.1 miles to where road turns left in Bradley.

4. Turn left on Old 37 and go 3 miles to where road turns.

5. Turn right, cross railroad tracks, then turn left.

6. After turning left, go six-tenths of a mile to S.R. 630.

7. Cross C.R. 630; name of road changes from Old 37 to Fort Green Road.

8. Go straight ahead on Fort Green Road for 4.1 miles to where road turns right.

9. Turn right, cross railroad tracks, then turn left.

10. Go straight ahead after turn for 5 miles to S.R. 664.

11. Turn left on S.R. 664 and go 4.7 miles to College Hill Road.

12. Turn right on College Hill Road and go 2.3 miles to S.R. 62.

13. Turn left on S.R. 62 and go 1.5 miles to Polk Road N.W.

14. Turn right on Polk Road N.W. and go 3.7 miles to C.R. 35A. (Polk Road N.W. becomes C.R. 35B before making turn on C.R. 35A.)

15. Turn right on C.R. 35A and go 4.1 miles to S.R. 64.

16. Turn left on S.R. 64 and go nine-tenths of a mile to Myrtle Street in town of Zolfo Springs. Myrtle Street is one block before U.S. Highway 17.

17. Turn right on Myrtle Street and go six-tenths of a mile to U.S. Highway 17.

18. Cross U.S. Highway 17 and continue on S.R. 66.

19. Go straight ahead on S.R. 66 for 23.2 miles to Sparta Road.

20. Turn left on Sparta Road and go 4.3 miles to Lakeview Drive.

21. Turn right on Lakeview Drive and go four-tenths of a mile to S.R. 17 (also Lakeview Drive).

22. Turn left on S.R. 17 and go seven-tenths of a mile to Kenilworth Lodge.

23. To resume route the next day, turn right out of Kenilworth Lodge and go four-tenths of a mile to C.R. 634.
24. Turn left on C.R. 634 and go one-tenth of a mile to Center Avenue.
25. Turn left on Center Avenue and go one-tenth of a mile to Lakeview Drive.
26. Turn right on Lakeview Drive and go 3.2 miles to Scenic Highway.
27. Turn right on Scenic Highway and go nine-tenths of a mile to Downing Avenue.
28. Turn left on Downing Avenue and go six-tenths of a mile to North Lake Sebring Drive, which later becomes Manatee Drive.
29. Go 1.1 miles from start of Lake Sebring Drive to Memorial Drive (C.R. 17A).
30. Turn right on Memorial Drive and go 3.6 miles to Main Street in Avon Park.
31. Turn left on Main Street and go 1.2 miles, cross U.S. Highway 27 and road becomes S.R. 64.
32. Go straight ahead on S.R. 64 for 12.4 miles and angle to right on S.R. 636.
33. Go 2.6 miles on S.R. 636 to Holland Town Road S.E.
34. Turn right on Holland Town Road S.E. and go 2.3 miles to Perdue Ranch.
35. Turn left at Perdue Ranch and go 1 mile to four-way stop.
36. Turn right at four-way stop onto C.R. 664B and go 2 miles to Jack Cliett Road.
37. Turn left on Jack Cliett Road and go 1 mile to C.R. 664A.
38. Turn right on C.R. 664A and road becomes C.R. 664B. Go 3 miles on this to County Line Road.
39. Turn left on County Line Road and go nine-tenths of a mile to Mount Pisgah Road.

40. Turn right on Mount Pisgah Road and go 5.7 miles, cross Peace River and angle slightly left to where it becomes Orange Avenue in Fort Meade.
41. Go straight ahead on Orange Avenue for 1.8 miles to U.S. Highway 98.
42. Cross U.S. Highway 98 and go eight-tenths of a mile to 9th Street.
43. Turn left on 9th Street and go one-half of a mile to U.S. Highway 17.
44. Turn right on U.S. Highway 17 and go 4.3 miles to C.R. 640.
45. Turn left on C.R. 640 and go 10.3 miles to Old 37.
46. Turn right on Old 37 and go nine-tenths of a mile and merge into S.R. 37.
47. Go 2.2 miles on S.R. 37 to end of route in parking lot.

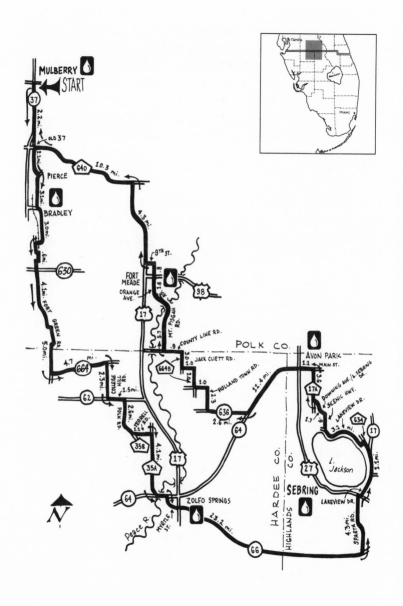

MULBERRY START
37
2.2 mi.
OLD 37
640 10.3 mi.
PIERCE
.3 mi.
5.1 mi.
BRADLEY
3.0 mi.
.6 mi.
630
4.1 mi. FORT GREEN RD.
5.0 mi.
664 4.7 mi.
2.3 mi. CHUBBS RD.
62 1.5 mi.
2.6 mi.
POLK RD.
TERRELL RD.
1.1 mi.
35B
4.1 mi.
35A
17
64
Peace R.
MYRTLE ST.
ZOLFO SPRINGS
23.2 mi.
66

9TH ST.
4.3 mi.
1.8
1.6
FORT MEADE
ORANGE AVE.
17
MT. PISGAH RD.
5.7
.9
COUNTY LINE RD.
664B
3.0 JACK CLIETT RD.
1.0
2.4
1.0
2.3
HOLLAND TOWN RD.
636
2.6 mi.
64
98
POLK CO.

AVON PARK
1.2 MAIN ST.
17A
3.6
DOWNING AVE./L. SEBRING DR.
SCENIC HWY.
1.7 .9
LAKEVIEW DR.
3.7 mi.
634
17
L. Jackson
27
SEBRING
LAKEVIEW DR.
4.3 mi.
SPARTA RD.
5.1 mi.
17
HARDEE CO.
HIGHLANDS CO.

12.4 mi.

N

245

▲ Everglades National Park loop

Everglades National Park is less than 50 miles from Miami, but a trip into that vast wilderness makes visitors feel as if they're a world removed from South Florida's largest city.

No bicycle tour of Florida would be complete without a ride through this park. It's 38 miles from the main entrance to the park near Florida City to the southern end at Flamingo, so those making the round trip in a single day would have a 76-mile ride.

Since the entire route is table-top flat, a round trip in a day is not too tough. But it really takes two days to appreciate what this 1.4 million-acre park is all about.

Getting to the park is simple. Take U.S. Highway 1 to Florida City, then transfer to State Route 9336. That road will take you to the park's main entrance and the visitor center. It's 11 miles from Florida City to the park entrance. Though the center is open only from 8 a.m. to 5 p.m. daily, the parking lot is open 24 hours a day, and you may park your car there overnight if you're planning to stay in Flamingo. Admission to the park for bicycles is $2; it's free if you're a senior citizen.

At Flamingo, the southernmost point on the United States mainland, you will have your choice of a lodge or campground. The charge at the latter is $4 per night for tents, and that includes use of facilities. It should be noted, though, that there's only cold water in the showers. Lodge fees vary according to the season with the higher rates in the winter. At any time of the year the price is more than your average motel. Cottages also are available, and they cost even more.

December through March are the good months. It's normally dry then in Florida, but when the weather heats

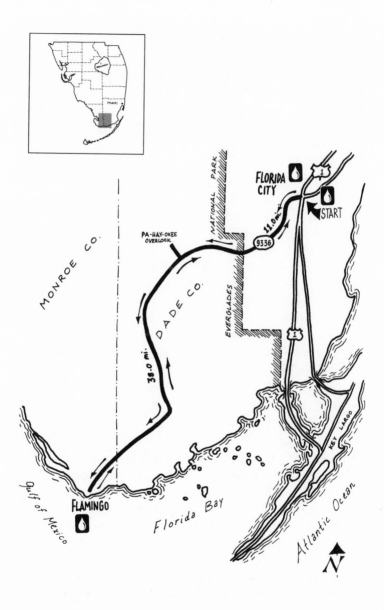

up and the rains arrive, the park is overwhelmed by vast clouds of mosquitoes. They almost can carry your tent off during the night. Camping is free during the summer months but you'll need gallons of bug repellent. Much of the park shuts down then because of the lack of visitors.

The Everglades is not without its problems, chief of which is the lack of fresh water. Nearby agricultural interests and the tremendous population boom in South Florida have created a heavy demand for water that has left life in the Everglades hanging by a thread. As you drive along S.R. 9336 on the approach to the park you'll pass many miles of fields that produce vegetables and fruits for much of the United States during the winter months. The demand for water here is extremely heavy.

The Everglades is the largest subtropical wilderness in the United States, and it's home to many endangered species of plants, animals and birds. More than 300 species of birds are found in the park, including such rare ones as the American bald eagle and the snail kite.

Other park residents include woodstorks, American crocodiles, manatees, otters and alligators.

It's estimated that about 30 Florida panthers, an elusive subspecies of lion, still live around the brush and hammocks in the park.

There are several ways to see and explore this great treasury of nature, but all of them may be best understood by stopping at the visitor center and seeing a short introductory film. That will give you an understanding of the size and unusual nature of this park.

From there you can pick and choose from a great variety of walking trails and bodies of water scattered throughout the park.

One of the most popular trails is the Anhinga. It's only a half-mile long, but it offers one of the best oppor-

Shark Valley, Everglades

tunities to see wildlife up close. Another well-visited site is the Pa-hay-okee Trail. This one is only a quarter-mile long and leads to an observation tower that offers a good view of part of the vast river of grass. The trails are equipped with boardwalks so you can observe the wildlife safely.

All along the road through the park you'll see lush forests and enormous sawgrass prairies. Many of the trees are cypresses that may be more than 100 years old. They look dead during the winter after losing their leaves, but they bounce back to life in early spring.

Early morning and late afternoon are the best times for bird watching, and some species that are rare or endangered throughout much of the world are relatively common in the park.

When you check into the visitor center, talk to one of the park service employees about the activities planned for that day. Naturalists give hikes, talks, canoe trips, tram tours, demonstrations and campfire programs during the year. There are schedules at the visitor center.

After you've reached Flamingo, stop by the marina if you're interested in boating. Small power skiffs, patio boats, houseboats and canoes can be rented there along with navigational charts. Tours at Flamingo also explore the mangrove wilderness and Florida Bay.

This park is a remarkable place. Actually it's a slow-moving fresh-water river that's 50 miles wide and a few inches deep that's fed by Lake Okeechobee. It creeps seaward through the Everglades on a riverbed that slopes gradually before finally emptying into Florida Bay.

Riding in the park is a real pleasure. The road is in good condition, and most of the traffic is moving slowly so the people in cars can get a close look at the surroundings. There are more than a dozen points of interest along the road where you can get off your bike to explore a trail or examine one of the many ponds. If you try to cram this whole trip down and back in a single day you won't get much of a chance to really see this remarkable park.

Remember, though, that the best time for visiting this park is in the winter. The mosquitoes in summer are far too plentiful to allow for full enjoyment of the Everglades.

One last reminder: Fill your water bottles when you leave the visitor center. It's a long 38 miles to Flamingo.

5.Safety

There is always a risk involved in bicycle touring — even when you're riding on quiet roads.

Florida leads the nation in biking fatalities and its record on bicycle safety is poor. With this in mind, here are a few suggestions on how to avoid accidents and injuries.

Four basic pieces of equipment will help protect you. They are:

A helmet. Almost 75 percent of all bicycle fatalities are the result of head injuries. Using helmets would have prevented many of these deaths. Tests show that a hard-shell helmet lined with a polystyrene mix effectively prevents head injuries.

Gloves. Using gloves protects the rider's hands in case of a fall and cushions them from handlebar vibrations.

A mirror. Using a rearview mirror — preferably one

attached to your glasses or helmet — will help you monitor traffic behind you.

Bright clothing. It's to the cyclist's advantage to be conspicuous. Bright clothing alerts motorists that you're on the road.

None of the routes in this book requires riding at night. Don't do it. About 60 percent of all adult fatal bicycle accidents in Florida happen during twilight and night hours.

The second most frequent cause of accidents is cyclists riding against traffic. Obey the law — ride on the right.

You'll encounter railroad tracks several times on these routes. Be sure to cross them at a 90-degree angle so the tracks won't trap your bike's front wheel and cause a fall.

Because all of these routes involve rural roads, there will be dogs — a few of them hostile. Stay calm and follow three basic rules: Tell the dog to go home; dismount, keeping the bike between you and the dog; squirt the dog with water from your water bottle.

And though it has nothing to do with safety, a lock is a good investment on a bicycle tour. Get the best you can afford. It still will be cheaper than buying a new bike.

Because many cyclists are confused about how Florida's laws apply to them, the more pertinent parts of the state statutes are reprinted here. They are listed as F.S. 316.3065 with the heading of Bicycle Regulations.

Every person propelling a vehicle by human power has all the rights and all of the duties applicable to the driver of any other vehicle.

A person operating a bicycle may not ride other than upon or astride a permanent and regular seat attached thereto.

No bicycle may be used to carry more persons at one time than the number for which it is designed or equipped, except that an adult rider may carry a child securely attached to his person in a backpack or sling.

No person riding upon any bicycle may attach the same or himself to any vehicle upon a roadway. This subsection may not prohibit attaching a bicycle trailer or bicycle semitrailer to a bicycle if that trailer or semitrailer has been designed for such attachment and solely for carrying cargo.

Any person operating a bicycle upon a roadway at less than the normal speed of traffic at the time and place and under the conditions then existing shall ride as close as practicable to the right-hand curb or edge of the roadway except under any of the following situations:

❑When overtaking and passing another bicycle or vehicle proceeding in the same direction.

❑When preparing for a left turn at any intersection or into a private road or driveway.

❑When reasonably necessary to avoid any condition, including but not limited to a fixed or moving object, parked or moving vehicle, bicycle, pedestrian, animal, surface hazard or substandard width lane that makes it unsafe to continue along the right-hand curb or edge.

Any person operating a bicycle upon a one-way highway with two or more marked traffic lanes may ride as near the left-hand curb or edge of such roadway as practicable.

Persons riding bicycles upon a roadway may not ride more than two abreast except on paths or parts of roadways set aside for the exclusive use of bicycles. Persons riding two abreast may not impede traffic when traveling at less than the normal speed of traffic at the time and place and under the conditions then existing and shall ride within a single lane.

Those who follow these regulations, stay alert at all times and have the recommended equipment should have no problems riding anywhere on the 40 routes in this book.

Have a nice ride!

Index